Heart of the Poppy

~ *From War to Amor* ~

Dan Irving

Dedicated to Amor Ministries

Acknowledgements

Heart of the Poppy could not have been written without the influence and special help of the following friends and contributors:

Scott Congdon, Wayne Kistner, Karen Irving, Gayla Congdon, Steve Horrex, Andy Lyde, Eric Miller, Cindy Young, Ken Young, Donald Richey, M.D., Pastor Lou Diaz, PhD., Pastor Will Wilson, Kenneth Prideaux-Brune, John Mitchell, Kevin Harvey, Simon Louagie, Hilary Geater Childs, Coleman Jennings, Cindy Barr, Andrea Wagner, The Evangelical Free Church of Chico, and Kathi Hiatt.

Contents

Forward

Rev. Dr. Lou Diaz
Lead Pastor
Evangelical Free Church of Chico

History is fascinating when related to something you know. The history of baseball. The history of jazz. The history of tea. History is especially alluring if it is tied to your own history. No wonder genealogy is a popular pastime of intrigue!

When you sleuth out how family history morphs into your own personal history, then you grow a deeper appreciation for the past efforts and accomplishments of your ancestors. You have a fascination about long-lost relatives who were famous or infamous. Sometimes you are able to discover a unifying theme or common trait even among the relics of your ancestors' divergent and dispersed descendants. Often you discover something revealing about your own identity.

Dan Irving has traced the "human family history" of a movement, or spirit of humankind, that has a propensity for helping fellow humans in need. Ironically, to see how compassionate and courageous this particular family tree is, one must see it in the historical context of war, injustice, and poverty. The worst settings seem to bring out the best actions from this Family of Saints.

Irving has a unique interest because he is related to these "ancestors" in two ways: He has known some of the main characters personally and he has joined their ranks. He is a historian and an activist. He has found the roots and the fruits of his own kind.

I first met Dan Irving when I stepped out of a thick fog in Mexico one early morning in 2006. My wife, Shirley, and I wanted to surprise the volunteer workers from the church where I had just been called to serve as their Pastor. Shirley and I drove down to San Diego and stayed the night before in a hotel and then, in the dark of pre-dawn, we sought out the Evangelical Free Church of Chico (EFCC) campground, distinguished by a large "big top" tent.

The fog was dense, and our visibility was barely one car-length in front of us. We crawled along in our vehicle at a snail's pace until we spotted an upright tent pole. As we entered the campground we encountered Dan Irving who was eating breakfast with Scott Congdon, one of the co-founders of Amor Ministries.

Dan and the rest of the EFCC volunteers were constructing homes for the poor and were surprised to see their new Pastor and his wife had driven twelve hours south from Chico, California, to not only surprise, but also to roll up their sleeves and work alongside their new parishioners.

Shirley and I spent the day helping to stucco the five houses the workers from EFCC had been building over a 4-day period for the homeless. Our clothes and shoes were so covered with "mud" that after we changed out of them at day's end, we discarded them in a trash bin as unusable.

Scott and Gayla Congdon had seen people living amidst trash in the garbage dumps of Mexico, and with Steve Horrex they had figured out a way to make homes for the homeless. Our church had participated in this effort by sending down groups for twenty years. Yet, no one had realized, including the founders of Amor Ministries that they connected to a movement reaching back in time to World War I. No one knew this incredible history, except for Dan Irving who had been mentored by Coleman Jennings. Dan was working on unravelling this mystery by connecting the dots, people, organizations and most importantly, relationships and how throughout this one-hundred-year story, the primary ingredient was faith in action.

Dan Irving, compelled by a passionate destiny, set forth to capture the origins of The Matriarch of the Movement: TOC-H. He studied books, interviewed people, traveled to historic sights, and mapped out a panoramic view, one panel at a time, so the inter-connectedness of each might be clearly seen.

The resulting mural you hold in your hands is at once a maze and amazing. Irving presents a storyline that appears to move in different directions but merges into something beautiful and beneficial for all humankind.

By stepping back in time, the reader is propelled forward to make a difference in these present times for the sake of the next generation. What had been paid forward is like a baton that we have received for us to pass on to others. We are carriers of the lantern, a lantern that guided Christians through the catacombs of Rome, one that shone light all the way back to the darkest hours of humanity.

Read this family history and be prepared to claim your roots and to live out your pedigree. History repeats itself both in atrocities and humanitarian efforts. Why not "act justly, love mercy and walk humbly with your God?" (Micah 6:8).

PART I

Chapter One

The Western Front

*"Even though I walk through the valley of the shadow
of death, I will fear no evil, for you are with me; your
rod and your staff they comfort me. You prepare a table
before me in the presence of my enemies. You anoint my
head with oil, my cup overflows. Surely goodness and
love will follow me all the days of my life, and I will
dwell in the house of the Lord."* Psalm 23: 4-6

You are going to die! It feels as if your death will arrive at any
time, within minutes, days, weeks—perhaps months. It appears
inevitable, inescapable. Your job is to kill. You watch your friends be
killed. You watch them suffer and die while you spend endless days
and nights in fear of being killed yourself. Your senses are numb, you
are surrounded by death. Its lifeless stare bores right through you. You
are haunted by it. The stench of death is everywhere, and it will never
leave you. Never! You cannot escape death's objective: to hunt you
down and destroy you, anyway possible. You would prefer a merciless
bullet to the brain. It would be quick and painless. For now, this is
your home, where the mud and blood flows together in the trenches on
the Western Front.

You are scared and even if you don't believe, you pray. You pray because it is the only thing you have words left for, the only thing which offers any hope. When the bombs fall thousands of soldiers "crawl-up" in their holes, wrapped in waterproof sheets, holding onto their Bibles. When there is nowhere to go, there is only one direction to turn.

You learn to live underground with rats the size of cats, only to surface when you are told. Told when to attack and kill or be killed. You live in waiting, always waiting. It's cold, it's wet, it's unbearably hot and at times it snows. Life can become insane and your sanity left   you a long time ago. The pain and the   suffering   are everywhere... and you struggle on, moment by moment, day by day, week by week. You no longer understand "Why?" because that doesn't change anything, and the reasons for you being here were lost a long time ago. Truth is, they never made any real sense at all.

In 1878 the Treaty of Berlin was agreed upon by the United Kingdom, Austria-Hungary, France, Germany, Italy, Russia   and the Ottoman Empire and it transferred control of Bosnia- Herzegovina to multi-ethnic   Austria-Hungary.   This   angered   Austria-Hungary's southern neighbor, Serbia as it desired to be united with fellow Serbs in Bosnia Herzegovina.

World War I was triggered by a Serbian terrorist group called The Black Hand who advocated violence for the creation of a better Serbia. They took orders from the head of the Serbian military intelligence, Colonel Dragutin Dimitrijevic, nicknamed "The Bull." Serbia felt threatened by Austrian-Hungary domination and The Black Hand meant to put an end to their rule. A group of seven young nationalists conspired to kill Archduke Franz Ferdinand, heir to the Austria-Hungary throne. They included a carpenter, a printer, a teacher and four students. Five were less than twenty years old, including Gavrilo Princip a Bosnian Serb. The only crime one of them was known to commit was striking a teacher. They were temperate, with several having never touched alcohol. None of them were gamblers. They were free of personal debts. However, they had one illness in common, tuberculosis. Fever can color the mind and they were destined for death, ready to die, and in their minds, heroically. They were inexperienced with no military training and armed with pistols, crudely made hand bombs and just in case, cyanide tablets for suicide. By any accounts their efforts should have been doomed to failure.

June 28th, 1914 was a beautiful day. The Serbian streets were filled with the celebration of the Feast of Saint Vitus, the symbol of Serbian resurrection: their victory over the Turks and the Ottoman Empire dating back to June 28, 1389. To the conspirators, it was the perfect day for their deadly mission. It was a time for Archduke Ferdinand to celebrate his fourteenth wedding anniversary with his wife, Sofie. Their marriage was a problem in the eyes of Emperor Francis Joseph because his nephew, the Archduke, married beneath his station in life. Sofie was the child of a noble from an obscure Czech family and was a lady in waiting to the Archduke's cousin, Isabella. The marriage was extremely unpopular and so unacceptable in the aristocratic circles of the Austrian-Hungary Empire, the Emperor abdicated any rank for their children. Sofie was routinely snubbed, ignored at the great court in Vienna and was not allowed to ride in the royal carriage or sit in the royal box. At court balls, where a royal procession was in order, Sofie was placed behind the last princess of royal blood and was not allowed to enter with her husband.

The Archduke was embittered by the official degradation of his wife. His life became riddled with broken friendships and he demonstrated angry tirades. To escape the humiliation of his royal life, Franz became an excessive hunter who by the age of forty-six bagged over 5,000 stags. He was the Inspector General of the Army and it was his duty to go to Sarajevo where the Austrian Army was holding annual maneuvers near the Serbian border. He longed for Sofie to enjoy the special honors he believed should be bestowed upon her and took her with him to celebrate their anniversary without the restrictions of the royal court back home.

To the Serbians, the Archduke represented a serious threat, he was heir to the throne and believed Slavs should be united, carrying an equal voice with the Germans. His voice would forever doom Serbia, never allowing the Serbs to rise as a great nation. There were four cars in the official procession of the Imperial Party, rolling through the unguarded streets on their way to visit the provincial governor. They passed the first conspirator who, with bomb in hand, froze. The second conspirator took aim at the Archduke's green feathers on his military helmet and threw his bomb right at him. The Archduke saw it coming, raised his arm to protect himself, deflecting the bomb onto the street where it rolled under the following vehicle and exploded, injuring a Count, a Countess and a Colonel along with bystanders. The procession sped away, passing three more of the assassins who just stood and did nothing.

Later that day, while the Archduke and his wife were on their way to the hospital to visit the wounded Colonel, the Archduke's chauffeur made a wrong turn. When the chauffeur realized his mistake, he stopped the vehicle to put it in reverse. Unbelievably, just six feet away stood Gavrilo Princip who did not hesitate. He pulled out his gun, stepped forward and fired two shots instantly killing the Archduke's wife, while mortally wounding the Archduke who died ten minutes later. Princip was arrested on the spot.

After the assassination the evidence of complicity was exposed by the conspirator's confessions and the imperial government of Austrian-Hungary determined there had to be grave consequences. One month later, on July 28th, Austria-Hungary declared war on Serbia. Then, within a week, the colossal collision of alliances, imperialism, militarism and nationalism escalated from the Balkan War into the First World War. A wrong turn, two rounds from a surprised assassin, two dead and the lynch pin had been pulled, catapulting the world into an avalanche of death, destruction and mayhem, the likes of which it had never seen before.

Truth is: peace is much more difficult to make than war. War can be started far too easily, and all too often begins without any realistic understanding of how it will ever end, if an end is what it is ever capable of coming to. The flash point started with the assassination, but in reality, it was just the spark igniting a brewing eruption. Now the most powerful nations on earth would have to do more than jockey for position, power and control, they'd have to fight for it, whether it was offensive to gain the upper hand or defensive to insure there wasn't a shift in the status quo.

Alliances formulated the sides. At the onset, it was the "Central Powers" also known as the "Triple Alliance" comprised of Austria-Hungary, Germany and Italy who would go to war if one of them were attacked. On the other side, it was the "Triple Entente" or the "Allied Powers" of France, Russia and the United Kingdom. France was to aid Russia and vice versa if either were attacked by Germany. Belgium neutrality had been guaranteed by a treaty between Britain and France with either coming to the aid of the other if their vital interests were threatened.

The alliances of allies were locked into place with the forces of the world already at great odds over issues of territory and power. Austria-Hungary, the weakest nation in Europe, needed to avenge the assassination of Ferdinand and declared war on Serbia—pushing the first domino over and setting everything in motion. Russia shared a common border with Austria-Hungary and sent a stern warning to desist from their action against Serbia. Austria-Hungary looked to Germany for support and Germany was all too ready and willing, and had been waiting for the opportunity to unleash their plans to propel the Fatherland as the dominant power in Europe.

The Schlieffen Plan was Germany's strategic offensive for achieving victory in fighting a war on two fronts: An Eastern Front with Russia and a Western Front with France. By all accounts, it was overly ambitious and simple. The plan was to concentrate troops in the west and quickly defeat France by taking Paris. Then relocate the bulk of the army via rail to the east to overwhelm the disorganized Russians before they could mobilize. Once Paris was taken, the French would be defeated and any Russian confidence against Germany would be broken, leaving them an easy enemy for the taking. Germany concluded after their conquest of Belgium, France and the Russian Empire they would ascend as the dominant leader in all of Europe. What Kaiser Wilhelm didn't understand or comprehend is the world just might resist Germany's onslaught, the world might just stand in the way and say "No!"

In 1871 Queen Victoria's British Empire covered one sixth of the world's geography. Queen Victoria was Kaiser Wilhelm's grandmother and died in 1901. By 1914 the British Empire had colonized and controlled one quarter of the world's population including Ireland, Australia, New Zealand, Canada, Hong Kong, the West Indies, India, Newfoundland, Labrador, Kenya, Nigeria, the African Gold Coast, Sierra Leone, Rhodesia and South Africa. Germany was united in 1871 and by 1914 was engaged in a naval arms race with Britain. Control of the seas meant control of the trade routes, the byways to ports, foreign goods and control of vulnerable countries. If you controlled the seas, you could control the world.

On August 4th, Germany plowed their forces into Belgium and from the onset civilians, women and children were part of the massacre in the "Rape of Belgium." From the German perspective, "It couldn't be helped." Germany calculated they would march straight through Belgium and would be celebrating Christmas in Paris. On the Eastern Front they began their attack against Russia. The massive invasion and violation of neutrality by the German army put the integrity of the existing alliances to the ultimate test. Mobilization of troops on one side led to mobilization on the other. It sucked in all the European and Russian powers, one right after the other quickly became consumed in the momentum of military mobilization. No side was backing down.

In Germany there was the initial atmosphere of jubilation, excitement and national pride. However, neutral Belgium did not completely oblige the troops from seven German armies as Belgium dug in with stiff resistance. While Belgium, France and Russia were attacked, Great Britain knew they would be next and declared war on Germany. It was the beginning of a new era, the time when Germany moved forward with aggression to expand her borders, her territory, all in the name of the "Fatherland."

The Ottoman Empire represented what is today known as Turkey. The culture and religion are primarily Islam and controlled by Sunni Muslims. On November 2, 1914 the Ottoman Empire entered the war on the side of the Central Powers, triggering internal hostilities between Muslims and Armenians. Muslims feared Armenians would sabotage their war efforts by siding and aiding the Russians. What followed is the first modern genocide with the systematic killing of Armenians, mostly through forced death marches where no food or water was given. The Muslim and Turkish massacre of Armenians did not discriminate between age or gender and included rape, torture, mass burnings, suffocation, starvation, poison and drownings. The Armenian Genocide by Turks and Muslims killed one to one and a half million Armenians and has never been officially recognized by the Turkish government.

The Germans began their offensive in August and were quickly successful in reaching the outskirts of Paris. Six French field armies and one British responded with an effective counter-attack known as the "Miracle of the Marne." The counter-attack not only stopped the

German offensive in their tracks, it forced the Germans to abandon their march on Paris and retreat, ending the mobilization of their grand offensive. The Germans then advanced north toward the sea, hoping to gain control of the channel ports. They were stopped at the First Battle of Ypres where an estimated 300,000 soldiers were killed, wounded or missing in action. To the Germans it became known as the "Kindermord bei Ypers"—the Massacre of the Innocents at Ypres. The advancing tide of German aggression had been stopped. The battle march Germany planned would last but a few months became apparent, it would be anything but brief and glorious. German parents mourned the death of their sons from every German university, the so-called bourgeois, the very best they had to offer were lying dead in mass, unmarked graves. The intoxication of German patriotism suddenly turned to disillusionment when the reality of death and destruction came so quickly to those so young.

At first it appeared to be a limited war between selected players: Austria-Hungary, Germany, Italy and the Ottoman Empire vs. Russia, France, Belgium and Britain. As the stakes rose, other nations realized any outcome would impact their security and the countries of the world took up sides. Between 1914 - 1918 more than one hundred countries from Africa, America, Asia, Australia and Europe would fight. It was billed as The Great War, The People's War, The Total War, World War I, and The War to End All Wars ...or so it was thought. Nobody perceived this would become one of the greatest stalemates and slaughters in the history of mankind.

Britain quickly deployed the British Expeditionary Forces (BEF) to Northern France and they dug in around Ypres, a small town in western Belgium with a population of 17,000. It was the Brits that led the heroic charge with their headstrong resolve of "May God Save the Queen" that challenged the Germans western border with Belgium in Flanders fields, where cities and towns like Antwerp, Bruges and Ypres are ancient battlegrounds soaked with blood from centuries of conflict.

The world dug in, literally, on both sides along what became the main theater of the war: "The Western Front;" a battle line 475 miles long, from the Atlantic Ocean to Switzerland with 6,000 miles of layered, systematic trenches. It would be life and death underground, towing the line on the Western Front for four miserable years, fortified by the expendable lives of soldiers.

Trench warfare: a new kind of horror with what appeared to be a never-ending flow of supplies made possible by industrial production. Each soldier could dig and remove one cubic foot of earth every three minutes and within thirty minutes a soldier could shovel enough dirt to create underground protection. Trenches were dug in rows with connecting rows upon connecting rows. New trenches were constantly excavated and there could be no sense of neatness or orderliness to this life. Soldiers were surrounded by dirt, and when it rained could be flooded out, and with the rain came the mud. If you were attacked and overcome, you would retreat, sometimes just a few meters back to another trench. Life and death between combatants in some areas was twenty-five yards wide, while in other areas it could be two to three hundred yards wide. The killing ground between opposing sides was appropriately named "No Man's Land."

Rank meant very little since the life expectancy for officers who led the front lines into battle was ten weeks. The infantryman carried an average load of sixty plus pounds: a rifle weighing ten pounds, a bayonet, entrenching tools, ammunition pouches holding a hundred rounds or more, a canteen, a large pack containing clothing, helmet, boots, field rations and emergency medical supplies. Their commanders—many of whom never visited the battle line—ordered countless blundering battle commands sending millions to their death.

Between the trenches in No Man's Land the battles, skirmishes, raids and sniping took place, leaving most of the dead and wounded between the lines. It was sheer torture for soldiers to listen to the suffering cries for help amongst the wounded, especially if he was your friend. Snipers took up tactical positions and waited, then opened up with a barrage of well-placed bullets killing many soldiers trying to retrieve their wounded mates.

Casualties for major battles ran into the hundreds of thousands on both sides, with calculations for victory being based on national birthrates to replace the losses. Battles raged and the death toll climbed: total dead in October 1914 - 80,000, November - 70,000. During the first four months of the war there were more than 800,000 casualties. Most deaths were amongst men in their early twenties: the youth of Europe.

The geography around Ypres is shaped like a rounded bowl known as a "salient." The "Ypres Salient" had an outer circumference of twenty miles, sloped up on three sides, north, east and south, like an amphitheater with Ypres being center stage. The Germans held the high ground on all three sides with the distinct advantage of attacking down on the British and her allies. It was an absolutely miserable piece of geography to try and hold, within easy range for the Germans to rain down shells and it was also vulnerable from naval bombardment. It made no tactical sense for the British to be entrenched on the underbelly of this Salient. However, the area represented the only piece of sovereign Belgium soil the Germans hadn't over-run. For the stubborn British and the allies who came to their aid, a heroic stand was made on this miserable piece of dirt, immobilizing much of the German army for almost the entire war.

The Ypres Salient became the focal point of the war, one that represented the absolute resolve and determination of the Allies, who at all costs were never going to give up, pullback or surrender. Many of the deadliest battles of the war were fought here including the First, Second, Third and finally, the Fourth Battle of the Ypres. During the Third Battle of Ypres more than four million shells were fired resulting in half a million casualties.

Just eight miles behind the British lines lay the small town of Poperinge which became a major supply depot where many soldiers escaped for time off from their living hell. Their routine was a week on the line, and if they survived, a week off. In 1914, the German Expressionist Otto Dix quickly came to terms with the landscape of the Western Front and described the stomach churning atmosphere as "lice, rats, barbed wire, fleas, shells, bombs, underground caves, corpses, blood, liquor, mice, cats, artillery, filth, bullets, mortars, fires, steel: that's what war is. It is the work of the devil."

Canadian army physician John McCrae wrote *In Flanders Field*, a poem which remains a lasting legacy of the terrible battle in the Ypres Salient in the spring of 1915.

In Flanders fields the poppies blow,
Between the crosses, row on row,
That mark our place; and in the sky the larks, still bravely singing,
Fly scarce heard amid the guns below.

We are the Dead.
Short days ago we lived, felt dawn, saw sunset glow,
Loved, and were loved, and now we lie in Flanders fields.

Take up our quarrel with the foe:
To you from failing hands we throw the torch;
Be yours to hold it high.
If ye break faith with us who die
We shall not sleep, though poppies grow in Flanders fields.

The trench lines barely moved for four years. Yet, as the beginning of this onslaught of death and destruction set in, the most incredible and wonderful thing happened, interrupting the war, if just for a day or two... Christmas! When stories of what took place circulated back home, the initial and official response was, "It didn't happen; it couldn't have happened." But happen it did on Christmas Day 1914. Death took a holiday and peace sprung forth in a spontaneous gesture from the hearts of men who desired goodwill towards one another, even if they were that bastard on the other side of No Man's Land.

After the war started, requests were made for a day of peace on Christmas Day including an appeal from Pope Benedict XV. The requests were quickly dismissed by the commanders and generals from both sides as "Impossible." What happened was amazing, although it was only a momentary aberration which had no consequences regarding the horror and devastation that lay ahead, yet it truly was a sign of what men and God desired: peace on earth.

The celebration of Christmas is deeply ingrained in German culture. It is the one holiday which brings everyone together, especially the family. German tradition and customs have greatly influenced and contributed to the world's celebration of Christmas with the Christmas Tree (Tannenbaum), Santa Claus (old St. Nicholas), the exchange of gifts, the Yule Log, the Christmas wreath, gingerbread and gingerbread houses, along with the collections of soldier nut crackers. Many of the cherished traditional Christmas Hymns sung around the world originated in Germany including Silent Night, O Tannenbaum, Ave Maria and Oh Christmas Tree.

The orders up and down the lines strictly forbid fraternization with the enemy. One was not supposed to get to know their opponent. It would disrupt morale and interfere with the offensive spirit within the ranks. The enemy was not your fellowman, he was different, a vicious entity set on death and destruction, one who must be stopped at all costs. He was consumed with evil, one you were to fight and defend against until the death. Each side concluded the other side was without a soul.

No one is certain exactly how or where it started. What history is certain of is that it started on Christmas Eve, December 24th, 1914. That night was a magical night along the lines with a sparkling, beautiful moon. The air was filled with frost and the North Star was in full view, just as it was almost two thousand years earlier, guiding three wise men to Bethlehem. That night of nights the moon was so bright you could see your own breath and it glowed with a blue phosphorous luminescence when one exhaled. On the lines around Ypres, the Germans were on one side and the Scottish, Brits and French on the other.

Part of it began with an incredible spectacle viewed across No Man's Land. The Germans placed small Christmas Trees, lit with candles along the top of their trenches. Rows and rows of them emerged from the enemy, the invaders; the ones who started the war; the ones who had no soul. Could this be a trick to lure soldiers out into the open, then open fire on them? But soon songs, sweet Christmas carols filled the night air and floated across the lines. Once a carol was completed, a round of applause was heard from the other side only to be followed by their own inspired worship song. One thing led to another and soon conversations were being struck up. A German shouts out, announcing a special gift is on its way and throws something across No Man's Land. Everyone dives for cover, only to be greeted by a boot filled with sausages and chocolates. The Tommie's (British soldiers) quickly compile their return gift: a Christmas card from Princess Mary along with Royal Christmas pudding. Then an invitation is called out, to meet in the middle and share some Deutche Schnapps. The Brits agree and say they'll meet in the penalty area, a footballer's term. Then... cautiously, with hope in their hearts and fear on their minds, they moved out to greet each other, not as enemies but as man to man in No Man's Land.

The risk was great, to leave oneself fully exposed on the field of battle. Yet, something deep inside those men overcame the war—it was Christmas! They decided to get together without permission or orders from the high command, to take the risk, to celebrate with each other, to forget the war, if only for a day or two. The word traveled quickly up and down the line. Messages carried by dogs and men shouting out the Good News. It spread like wildfire. It was spontaneous and agreed upon by the men, "You no shoot, we no shoot day." The following morning on Christmas Day placards of "Merry Christmas" could be seen on both sides. Slowly they came out, up and down the trench lines and soon No Man's Land was filled with soldiers. Gifts were exchanged, and they sang Good King Wenceslaus, Home Sweet Home, God Save the King, Auld Lang Syne and Oh Holy Night. The Germans proudly sang "Dies ist der Tag, den Gott gemacht - This is the Day the Lord Had Made." When they sang Silent Night together, everyone sang the words in their own language. It was a beautiful chorus of different words meaning the same thing. Men stayed awake the entire night. It was the most beautiful night of the year.

They took the opportunity to collect and bury the dead. Each side helped the other remove the corpses, dig the graves and bury the fallen. Chaplains conducted funeral services. They saluted each other and respected the fact that although they differed as to why they were there, they recognized they had all been drawn into something beyond their control and it made no difference which side you were on as death has no boundaries.

There was one soldier who refused to participate in what was taking place. He was a young baptized Catholic who fled to Bavaria to escape Austrian conscription at the beginning of the war and scratched out a meager living painting scenes on post cards. When Germany invaded Belgium he volunteered to enlist and eight weeks later was in Flanders, not far from Ypres, as a field messenger with the 16th Bavarian Reserve Infantry Regiment. He was a Corporal, short with a dark, thick, ominous mustache. His name was Adolf Hitler and they called him "Adi." When Hitler learned of what was taking place, he was angry and refused to participate in the celebration of Christmas and retreated far behind the lines. He argued with his fellow soldiers, "Have you no German sense of honor left at all?" Hitler would have nothing to do with his own unit's celebrating in a monastery with a reading of the Christmas Gospel by a soldier, a Lutheran theology student, who like Hitler had been decorated with the Iron Cross. Hitler would have nothing to do with this celebration of the birth of the Savior, even though he was Catholic. As a soldier he received no mail, no parcels, never spoke of family or friends, didn't smoke, drink or socialize and often, just sat alone.

An impromptu orchestra formed with trumpets, a violin and accordions. There were bicycle races on bikes without tires found in the ruins of a house. Games of football broke out on the broken ground littered with shell holes, ditches and barb wire. However, with a strong desire to play, footballers can play on almost any terrain with some imagination. Stretchers were set up as goal posts, caps were set aside as field markers and spectators spread two deep along the sidelines with rifles flung over their shoulders. In some of the games, hundreds of soldiers took part. The games were utter chaos with everyone trying to have a go at the ball. Soldiers played in their boots in the mud with no referees, but there were no purposeful fouls, just good-natured sport.

German Lieutenant Johannes Niemann recorded the event in his diary and viewed something he wondered about. "At this soccer match our privates soon discovered that the Scots wore no underwear under their kilts so that their behinds became clearly visible any time their skirts moved in the wind. We had a lot of fun with that, and in the beginning, we just couldn't believe it... I myself got a private lesson one time when I was seriously wounded and lay on the floor of a British ambulance, with four lightly wounded Scotsmen sitting on a supporting bar right above me."

When the high command learned of what was taking place they were infuriated. What were they going to do, court-martial entire regiments? No. What they did was order renewed hostilities, along with threats to officers to assure fighting would resume. No newspaper in Britain would print the story. For the folks back home, it was incomprehensible to understand what these men were experiencing and how could they, even for a day or two, give death a holiday.

Brigadier Walter Congreve, Commander of the 18th Brigade reported, "It was the men who had arranged a truce betwe themselves and all day long they have been walking about singin smoking. The officers also walked and smoked, even to a Colonel." The high command ordered for firing to recommence at midnight. Everyone returned back to their hole in the ground, back to the war, while the air resonated all around until midnight with the continuous singing of "Silent Night, Silent Night, all is well, all is right, round yon Virgin mother and child, holy infant so tender and mild. Sleep in heavenly Peace, Sleep in heavenly peace..." At midnight, the bombardment started back up and they were at it again.

❀

The Germans developed a new killing agent, chlorine gas, which caused death by stimulating the over production of fluid in the lungs, resulting in drowning from the inside out. Six thousand cylinders, each weighing ninety pounds, containing 160 tons of chlorine gas were hand carried to the front lines. At 5:00 p.m. on April 22, 1915, during the Second Battle of Ypres, the cylinders were opened into a light prevailing east-west breeze, blowing the grayish-green clouds toward the Allies trenches. The heavier than air gas followed the contours of the earth, sinking into the trenches, forcing soldiers to abandon their protective positions, out into the open, exposing them to enemy fire. Within ten minutes, 6,000 were dead and thousands blinded. The soldier's choice: breathe the gas and drown from the inside out or expose oneself to the enemy. In many instances the result was the same: death.

Soldiers stumbled to the rear, clutching their throats, coughing, gagging and suffocating. Within an hour most of the front line was abandoned, opening a gap 8,000 yards wide. The Germans attacked and started to break through but a division of Canadian and British troops under the suffocating conditions—the likes of which they had never experienced, counterattacked despite the gas and the line was retaken and held.

The Germans continued to use gas throughout the war and later would include the deadlier asphyxiate, phosgene gas and then mustard ... blistered away tissue, inside or out. Without a gasmask, the re was to urinate in your handkerchiefs and breathe th to help neutralize the effect until the gas dispersed. 'ive use of gas warfare during World War I was just a the Holocaust: Adolf Hitler and Nazi Germany's final solution to their demonic Jewish question—industrial gas extermination.

For three years the battle lines remained stationary. It snowed, it rained, the trenches filled up with mud and men drowned. Each side learned how to maintain and defend their entrenched positions, while neither side was capable of breaking through the others'. British General Douglas Haig was in command of all British forces along the Western Front with his headquarters safely behind the lines, protected from the battle lines he never visited. Haig never witnessed the death and destruction where 250 to 300 men were dying daily. To him the war was but a distant thunder.

During the daily struggle of life and death and the devotion to each other to stay alive, deep bonds of friendship were formed. Only the soldiers in the trenches knows, from day to day, moment to moment, what they were experiencing. Only his friends in the trenches can relate to such an environment. Others can read about it, even write about it, but no outsider could ever come close to imagining what it was really like. C.S. Lewis was nineteen years old when he volunteered in the Somerset Light Infantry. He experienced trench warfare and was wounded by friendly fire. Lewis became a famed Christian author who wrote The Chronicles of Narnia along with fifty other books. Lewis expressed a great disliking for those who from a distance thought they understood life on the front, and with ease and safety issued advice and exhortations.

By the end of 1916 over one million soldiers were dead, yet the resolution of the German people remained strong and in their mind, they had something to show for it. Germany was occupying all of Belgium, with one exception, the area around Ypres. They occupied northern France, Russian Poland and there was the defeat of Serbia and Romania. Germany believed they were winning the war, although the cost of waging the war was impacting everyone back home. Everyone had to sacrifice, and for every German living in the Fatherland no meal was filling, homes couldn't be heated, clothes couldn't be replaced and new shoes were nonexistent. Sixty percent of wage earning men were entrenched at the front lines and families were dependent upon a small state allowance that was insufficient to cover the basic costs needed to sustain them. But until the end, Germans cried out "Durchhalten" for "See it through!"

The principal causes of death in this modern mechanized war came from the industrial killing machines being used for the first time: tanks, heavy artillery, flame throwers, submarines and U boats (Underwater Boats). As long as the materials and supplies were provided, the machines would operate with one objective: death and destruction. Predominately, in one form or another, it was artillery, from a field mortar to the 1,800-pound shells of Big Bertha that did most of the killing. The science of warfare grew like an explosion within itself leading to bigger and more accurate explosions. Massive amounts of artillery were deployed. At 4:00 a.m. on March 21, 1918 the Second Battle of the Somme began with a massive storm of coordinated Allied fire from 6,608 artillery guns and 3,534 trenched mortars.

The mass slaughter of men at an unprecedented rate rendered the soldier in the trench an insignificant and replaceable commodity. However, the chivalry of the war, exploited by the media took place in the air when the skies opened to a new type of warfare: aerial warfare, capturing the public imagination and their desire for good sporting matches between combatants. The daredevils of the sky defied gravity with the adventure of the conflict romanticized in the newspapers back home, along with bringing national pride to the men on the fields of battle. Initially, the importance of the airplane was for observation and reconnaissance. Its use advanced with the ability to drop bombs by hand until release mechanisms were built. Pilots strafed the troops on the ground with machine gun fire. The minimum age for pilots was seventeen and a country background riding horses was considered the best indicator for being a good pilot while the life expectancy for rookie pilots was ten days. It was a new dimension of war, a dimension the world had never experienced before, a dimension that rained terror from the skies when Germany attacked England with the first indiscriminate air attacks on civilian populations.

In 1915, German engineers synchronized the propeller movement of the German Faulkner to the machine gun where bullets were geared to fire directly between the spacing of the propeller blades. Captain Manfred von Richtofen, the Red Baron had eighty kills to his name when he was finally shot down by rifle fire during the Third Battle of Ypres. This German slaughter in the air continued until the Allies copied the synchronized technology into their own aircraft.

The battle in the air would not determine the outcome of the war but it gave each country a new-found way to glorify and illustrate the war. It was the fighter pilots who became the symbols and heroes of the war with more than 50% of the 22,000 trained British and German pilots becoming casualties. While appearing sporty with a sense of gamesmanship the reality remained, aerial combat was a deadly affair. Allied pilots were not issued parachutes because the high command concluded many would bailout too early. Instead, if the end became inevitable, they had been issued revolvers for a bullet through the brain.

The American invention from the Old West of barbed wire was used extensively to fortify and entangle offensive efforts with thousands of miles of coiled wire protecting the trenches. Behind the wire sat machine guns with sweeping capabilities of rapid fire which easily mowed down advancing soldiers. The Germans suspected the Brits had developed a mechanized rapid-fire rifle, enabling the outnumbered British troops to defend against German advances. The reality was no such thing, other than solid military training, marksmanship and discipline in the operation of British riflery. Seasoned riflemen of the British forces can deliver steady, accurate fire of up to eighteen rounds per minute.

When the war started, armies were somewhat Napoleonic in nature with horses and mules pulling equipment. Britain called up 165,000 mounts for their cavalry, Serbia-Austria 600,000 mounts, 715,000 for the Germans and for Russia, over a million. In all, the ratio of horses to men throughout the war was one horse for every three men.

In 1915 during the first months of Germany's unrestricted naval campaign, 227 British ships were sunk, mostly by German U-Boats. Britain ruled the seas until the German U Boat turned the tables and drove Britain to its most notorious land offensive—the Third Battle of Ypres with the objective of destroying the German submarine bases along the Belgian coast. To commence the attack, the British lined up 2,266 guns along a seven-mile front with each gun just five yards apart, ten times the normal density for an offensive barrage. The nonstop bombardment of shelling lasted for fifteen days and included 425 million shells. Throughout the bombardment it rained, softening the ground to liquid mud, turning it to quicksand. The bombardment ended on June 7th at 3:50 a.m. when General Haig ordered ground troops and 136 tanks to move forward into the pouring rain. The heavy tanks got stuck in the mud and when soldiers dove into the craters for protection, they were engulfed in it. They couldn't crawl out as the mud sucked them down turning the craters into human burial grounds.

Attacking the German stronghold known as "The Flanders Position" had devastating consequences. Here the German lines were nine layers thick with a front line of listening posts, three lines of sheltered battalions, followed by a battle zone consisting of machine guns strategically placed in concrete pillboxes. The last reserves were the "Reward Zone," where counter attack units waited safely behind concrete bunkers.

Of the actual battle, Officer Edwin Vaughan of the Royal Warwickshire Regiment wrote, "From other shell holes from the darkness on all sides came the groans and wails of wounded men; faint, long, sobbing moans of agony, and despairing shrieks. It was too horribly obvious that dozens of men with serious wounds must have crawled for safety into new shell holes, and how the water was rising about them, and powerless to move, they were slowly drowning. Horrible visions came to me with those cries, of men lying maimed out there trusting their pals would find them, and now dying terribly, alone amongst the dead in the inky darkness. And we could do nothing to help them."

The ground was so wet and soft, shells falling from the sky would land unexploded, buried in the mud. Even to this day, unexploded ordinances remain hidden and submerged in the fields of Flanders where poppies grow. The battled lasted three months with the first phase being nothing but mud and blood. During August, the British were ordered to attack on six separate occasions, barely gaining any ground while 60,000 British casualties were sustained. Whoever first said, "War is Hell" knew what they were talking about. By the time the offensive of the Third Battle of Ypres ended, only a few miles of ground had been gained. The estimated casualties and dead: 800,000. It was one of the greatest slaughters in history and for the Allies it represented a gain of two inches for every dead soldier. Five months later, the Germans recaptured every inch of ground taken without any resistance.

The landscape was devastated from the bombings. All vegetation, trees and growth were annihilated. What was left was a ground covering of death and destruction, potted with all sizes of craters. It truly was "No Man's Land." Nothing here could survive the constant bombardment of industrial explosions of every kind known to man. Amazingly, out of this chaos, something would spring forth. Something which would come to symbolize this horrific conflict: a flower; a bright, dark red, flower: the poppy. Fields of poppies, sprouting up in life throughout the fields of death and destruction. A simple, red, passionate flower, representing all the blood spilled, yet, vibrant enough to overcome the death and destruction, and offer hope and a new life.

In the end, it was the Americans and submarines that broke the impasse. When Germany declared unrestricted warfare on the high seas and ordered their U-boats to attack military and merchant vessels, sinking any vessels at will without warning in international waters, America's commerce and security interests were being sunk in the open seas. In 1914 the United States was not a military power and during the first three years of the war, President Woodrow Wilson remained determined that "This was Europe's war," although the U.S. supported Britain and France with needed resources and supplies. The United States stayed out even after German U-boats sank the British passenger liner *RMS Lusitania*, killing 1,198 including 128 American passengers on May 7th, 1915. Germany claimed the Lusitania was a military vessel carrying military cargo. Britain and America denied the claim saying the Lusitania was strictly carrying passengers. Decades later, when the sunken ship was explored, Germany's claims were confirmed. President Wilson demanded for Germany to put an end to the sinking of passenger ships. Germany not wanting America to enter the war, initially complied.

On January 16, 1917 Britain's secret cryptography group, "Room 40" intercepted and decrypted the famed "Zimmerman Telegram," representing Germany's invitation for Mexico to join the war and attack the United States. By doing so, Mexico could reclaim much of the territory previously lost to the United States in 1850. On January 31st, Germany again declared unrestricted U-boat warfare and would sink military or merchant vessels on the open seas. Three American merchant vessels were sunk. The Zimmerman Telegram was published on March 1st and the American public was outraged. Woodrow Wilson's resolve to stay out of the war was broken and on April 6th

Congress Declared War on Germany. The United States would not formally join the Allied Powers but joined as an "Associate Power."

President Wilson's family were friends with the prominent Hennen Jennings family in Washington, D.C. Hennen's son, Coleman spoke fluent French, had graduated from Harvard University and was enrolled at Harvard Law School. When the war started, he dropped out of Law School to volunteer for the army, was promoted to 1st Lieutenant in the Aviation Section of the Signal Corps and was with the earliest deployment of the American Expeditionary Forces (AEF) to France in 1917. Jennings was assigned to General John J. Pershing who commanded all the American troops in France.

It wasn't as if the U.S. cavalry was ready to charge in and save the day because back then, the United States military didn't have a cavalry. The military consisted of an army of 100,000 poorly trained soldiers and 10,000 well trained Marines. After "War!" was declared, America drafted four million men and the "Doughboys" (a term originating from the Mexican-American War where American soldiers fried flour dumplings—doughnuts) were on their way. Most American troops would not arrive until 1918.

The initial German response to the Americans entering the war was voiced by Admiral Capelle, the Secretary of the State for the German Navy, "They will not even come, because our submarines will sink them. Thus, America from a military point of view means nothing, and again nothing and for a third time nothing."

What the U.S. had was a substantial navy, the second largest fleet in the world of modern battleships, destroyers and submarines. With mobilization of the U.S. Navy the balance of naval power in the Atlantic and North Sea immediately changed in favor of the Allies. Germany was now confronted by a new realization, the U.S. Army and Marines on land, and the U.S. Navy at sea.

By 1918 there had been massive death toll on the Western Front and wartime fatigue was epidemic. Germany's manpower and resources were dwindling and now, more than three years after the war started, the United States would be sending 10,000 fresh troops daily to France. Not only did the United States enter the war, they became the inevitable deciding factor that put an end to the fighting. They brought renewed hope to the Allies and the Front, and with them came the American Spirit, that uniquely American focus of single minded purpose, coupled with a lighthearted sense of humor. It was just what the Allies needed.

By May 1918, America had arrived with over one million troops, half of them being deployed to the front lines. The Marines landed and immediately held their own with tenacity. On June 2nd during the Battle of Belleau Wood, Marines fought and denied the Germans access to the road towards Rheims. If the Germans gained access to Rheims, they would be able to double their offensive capacity in supplying their troops. Company Commander, Captain Lloyd Williams of the 5th Regiment led his troops into the battle. He was met by retreating French forces and a French Major who ordered him to retreat as well. At that moment, one of the finest responses of the American military spirit was made when Captain William's answered: "Retreat!? Hell, we just got here." Captain Williams died from his wounds during the battle. Today, the 2nd Battalion of the 5th Regiment is the most highly decorated battalion in the Marine Corps with their motto: "Retreat, Hell!"

Once the hackles of the United States were raised, there was no turning back and for Germany, the end of their misguided aggression was at hand. A new bombardment against the Germans started on September 28th and for every shell the Germans launched over the line, the Allies returned twenty, with 945,052 ordinances being unloaded within two days, a mind shattering five plus shells fired every single second. France and Britain were down to their last reserves and the Germans were barely holding on.

Russia was ruled by Czar Nicholas II who was the Emperor of Russia, the King of Poland and the Grand Duke of Finland. Russia withdrew from the Eastern Front in 1917 with the start of the Russian Revolution resulting in a civil war that would not end until 1923, ending the autocratic rule of the Russian monarchy and which led to the creation of the Soviet Union.

With historical hindsight, how often are men blindly led into battle, motivated by national pride while remaining ignorant of the actual circumstances and the cost? How often has the world been led into war by well-intended foolish leaders, whether by imperial rule, dictatorship or even democracy, only to learn they were wrong, dead wrong? Who pays the price, the ultimate price? The battlefields of history are littered with those who pay that price with their lives, their limbs and their sanity, including innocent civilians, wherever the line is drawn. The youth of nations killed off. And for their loved ones, they will never again share the light of day with their sons, husbands, brothers, cousins and boyfriends. In the end, World War I could only be embraced by a temporary peace, an armistice agreed to when the expenditure of life and the costs of financing such a pursuit were determined by the powers to be expendable no more.

What could Germany do? They had lost the best of their youth, morale was non-existent and now the Americans were deploying millions of new troops. After four years of war, the Germans had destroyed the Czar of Russia's army, defeated the Italians and Romanians, had been successful in demoralizing the French and fought the British to a stalemate however Germany had exhausted their ability to resupply the front lines with new troops and realized they could no longer survive more fatalities. Germany had run out of their single most nonexpendable resource: men. They were being defeated through attrition and pure exhaustion. By 1918 the Germans were done. The BEF captured 188,700 prisoners and 2,840 big guns, the French captured 139,000 prisoners and 1,880 guns while the newly arrived Americans captured 43,300 prisoners and 1,420 guns. Even the Belgian army captured 14,500 prisoners and 474 guns. The German army was no longer losing, they were giving up.

Germany retreated to their last position of resistance, "The Hindenburg Line," most of which followed the original trench line of 1914. There would be no victory for anyone. The death toll: 1,700,000 French, 1,500,000 soldiers and civilians from the Austrian-Hungary Empire, 2,000,000 Germans, 460,000 Italians, and many hundreds of thousands of Turks and over a million Armenians as their numbers were never counted. For the British, over a million were dead, half a million bodies were never found and there were millions wounded and scarred for life. Today, throughout Belgium and France are the graves and memorials to the fallen. In France, at the Thiepval War Memorial are the names of 73,367 British and South African soldiers who died at the Battle of the Somme who have no known graves. For the Americans who arrived late in the war, the death toll was 117,000.

Thirty-six percent of all the young men born in Europe from 1892-1895 were dead, more than a third of all the young men from Russia, Serbia, Germany, France, Belgium and Britain were gone. The conservative estimate from 1914 – 1918 is sixty-five million men took up arms, ten million died including civilians and more than twenty million were mutilated and wounded.

On November 18, 1918, in the eleventh month, at eleven minutes past the eleventh hour, the guns fell silent. The Peace Conference officially opened in Versailles, France on January 18, 1919 with delegations from thirty-seven different nations. However, because of the Russian Revolution, no delegates from Russia attended.

It was the most powerful nations on earth working to protect the world against future unbridled aggression, insuring this would be the last war, the War to end all Wars. President Wilson took the lead with a peace plan of fourteen points he hoped would be honorable to all combatants. Accompanying the President to Versailles as an aide-de-camp (personal assistant) was Coleman Jennings who was awarded the Chevalier Legion of Honor, France's highest decoration. Initially, there was excitement and enthusiasm behind Wilson's peace proposal and for a League of Nations to prevent future wars. Wilson succeeded in obtaining consent amongst the Allies to territorial divisions respecting self-determination.

A treaty was signed on June 23, 1919 in the Hall of Mirrors, a prophetic setting for a complicated, compromising agreement that unless enforced would bring anything but peace. President Wilson was awarded the Nobel Peace Prize, however the U.S. Senate refused to ratify the agreement and the United States never joined the League of Nations.

The terms of the Treaty were harsh, but not harsh enough, and they were not vigorously enforced. Germany remained intact and was not mortally wounded. During the peace process, Germans felt humiliated by Britain and France who were punitive in their demands. The Allies were unable to agree on the total amount of restitution Germany would pay and made the blundering mistake of postponing such determination until 1921 with Germany having to pay five billion dollars in the interim. The postponement of war guilt led to brewing consternation and embitterment, adding insult to injury for the prideful Germans who said they were *"stabbed in the back."* With America's absence from the newly formed League of Nations it was impotent in deterring future aggression. Incongruously, Germany disregarded their offensive war and viewed themselves as the victims.

The Armistice stopping World War I was nothing more than a recess from hostilities. The world exhausted from the   stalemate, agreed to take a break. In reality, that's all it was. It was hoped the Versailles Treaty, with all its faults would contain enough substance to sustain the cessation of hostilities. However, this peace without victory was fragile and doomed to failure without the full cooperation of Britain, France and the United States. The treaty had to be vigilantly enforced which was not the case. In competition, whether it be a chess match, or a good sporting event, unresolved conflict or stalemates only sets the stage for a greater rematch.

The ongoing humiliation of the prideful Germans was fueled by one of the most gifted and inspiring public speakers the world has ever heard: Adolf Hitler. The loser needed someone to blame, someone from within. That infection of resentment and German national anger found its target in the Jewish race. Hitler's accession to power commenced in 1933 when Germany raised an even uglier head, the Schutzstaffel, the SS whose symbol was a skull and cross bones known as the "Death Head." They operated as Hitler's personal body guard, opened and operated the first Nazi concentration camp at Dachau in 1933, just fourteen years after the Armistice. Twelve hundred more concentration camps would follow, becoming the social, religious and economic dumping ground for those determined by Hitler and his evil empire to be inferior, unacceptable and not of pure Germanic blue blood.

By 1939 Hitler was the Leader of the Third Reich and ordered the invasion of Poland starting World War II. It would not be until towards the end of World War II when the flames and roar of the German crematoriums and Germany's systematic killing of Jews, Soviet POWs, the disabled, blacks, homosexuals, Jehovah's Witnesses, Roman Catholics, Poles, Gypsies and Freemasons would come to the world's attention; after six million had been gassed and put to death. Finally, the long-standing World at War that started from a spark in 1914 came to an end in 1945. The combined death toll of both wars is staggering and incomprehensible: seventy to eighty million lives, with the greatest percentage of those deaths occurring amongst civilians.

It is impossible to comprehend the overwhelming loss of life. Perhaps, Laurence Binyon says it best in his poem *For the Fallen:*

They shall grow not old, as we that are left grow old:
Age shall not weary them, nor the years condemn.
At the going down of the sun and in the morning
We will remember them.

.

Chapter Two

Tubby

"Sermons may edify, but they seldom change a man. The thing which does change a man, is to watch some other man doing something which cannot be explained, except upon the basis that he loves the cause of God."
Tubby Clayton

Just as the miracle of Christmas was celebrated along the Western Front there was soon to be another miracle to arrive, one that was short in stature but walked tall and radiated the hope of Christ. This man of God who brought hope, laughter, peace, humanity and Christ to the war zone would go on to create one of the most prolific post war movements the world has ever known. A man who saw visions and who had the practical and common sense to translate them into action; a man whose sympathy towards others was boundless and who inspired others to help him by trusting in them.

His name was Philip Thomas Byard Clayton and his ancestors originated in the North of England during the early sixteenth century around Newcastle with a reputation for being eccentric and anything but dull. They spread throughout England as merchants, politicians and sailors including the famed Captain Thomas Byard whose family united with the Claytons through marriage. His nickname was "Brave Byard" and his men adored him, King George III's enemies feared him and songs were written about his adventures at sea during the 18th

Century. As legend would have it, he was said to have died of a broken heart because when this sea salt grew old, they wouldn't let him fight any more.

By the beginning of the seventeenth century members of the Clayton family were living on Tower Hill in London. They operated a prosperous family business as merchants in naval supplies. It was the pews at All Hallows Church, the oldest church in London, where the family knelt and gave thanks to the Almighty. When England struggled with civil war and recovered under the Commonwealth, the Claytons were wise and careful to apply the Cromwellian understanding of "Trust in God," and "Keep your powder dry."

Through generations of Claytons came the Reverend Samuel Clayton who achieved a significant amount of financial and political success. He was respected and never let his success pollute his soul. He had four sons, his eldest being Reginald, who with his brothers attended Marlborough College, in Wiltshire. The school was founded in 1843 by clergymen and the Archbishop of Canterbury who desired to start a boarding school for sons of the cloth. The school was wrought with discipline and physical abuses carried out by the headmaster and instructors on their captured audience: the students. Reginald, his brothers and other students defied the authorities and rebelled. For three days and nights these boys of Marlborough took over the campus and resisted the pleas, threats and physical assaults in what is known as the school's "Great Rebellion." To squelch the rebellion the authorities called in the local police. The stress was too much and afterwards, Reginald was unable to continue his studies and became seriously ill with what was commonly referred to at the time as "brain fever." His doctors were convinced further academic study would be too much of a strain and did what most English physicians did for patients who could afford it and recommended a change of climate.

Reginald was sent off to Queensland in Northern Australia which was being pioneered by the British. His only reservation in leaving home was saying goodbye to his true love, his cousin Isabel Shepard. Prior to his departure, he and Isabel met and pledged their undying fidelity and love to each other. He was sixteen and she was twelve.

After spending ten years pioneering the Northern Australian bush, Reginald had become a man. He saved enough money to return home to England and claim his bride. They were married, and the newlyweds traveled back to Queensland and began to raise a family. Isabel gave birth to two sons while she managed their home in the land of endless horizons. On December 12, 1885, Isabel gave birth to their third son, Philip Thomas Byard Clayton, named partially after Captain Thomas Byard, and as fate would have it, they both possessed the same stubborn courage in the face of war.

The following year, Queensland suffered one of the longest droughts in the history of Northern Australia. The Claytons decided to take a break from the heat and returned home to England to introduce their sons to family, along with making the necessary arrangements for the boys' education. Reginald had worked hard and managed to save the incredible sum of L25,000 which he deposited in the Queensland banks. For the trip home, they departed with L800 in their pockets. During their visit the Queensland drought ended and was followed by torrential rains, flooding immense areas and washing away what so many worked so hard for. The drought, then the rains and a massive flood destroyed the regional commerce including the collapse of the local banks. British colonists, including Reginald, lost everything.

At forty-two it is difficult for a man to start over. Yet, Reginald had learned by experience what perseverance, dedication and hard work can accomplish. He had done it in the Australian bush, and with only L800 to his name and a family to feed, he would do it again, however this time it would be in London. Twenty years later, Reginald was able to retire with a stable income.

Philip Clayton, although born in Australia was a British subject who grew up with traditional English schooling. He was short and pudgy, and his school mates coined him the nickname "Tubby," a name that became endearing to all who knew and loved him. As a schoolboy, Tubby learned the importance of a good laugh, especially when it could be used to defuse a difficult situation. He became so adept with humor, he was able to incorporate laughter within the decorum of the classroom in such a way as not to upset the deportment of the class or his teachers while gaining the respect and admiration of his fellow classmates.

Although Tubby attended Oxford University, he became more interested in individuals and personalities than in books or academics. Tubby said he learned more from his observations of men on the

streets than he ever learned from any book or classroom. While at
Oxford, he learned to smoke a pipe along with acquiring a taste for
good Cognac. His college resolve was to see and do everything and to
have a good time along the way, the common pursuit for the youth of
any generation. Tubby was a quick study, learned the futility of foolish
pleasures and became very selective in his pursuits.

Initially, young Tubby began his study of theology with the notion
he was going to disprove it. Later, Tubby confessed it was a dangerous
experiment as he became convinced by the truth of the Gospel. As for
his total conversion of heart and mind, Tubby declared "The evidence
was too good." Not only did Tubby become convinced by the truth of
Christianity, he graduated at the top of his class in Theology.

While attending Oxford, Tubby learned his most important lesson
in the art of social service. On occasion, a physician by the name of
Doctor John Stansfeld visited Oxford. Doctor Stansfeld was a man
dedicated to those in need. He ran a boy's club in the poorest section
of South London and devoted himself to providing free medical care
for those who couldn't afford it. Stansfeld believed life had a purpose
and part of his purpose was to penetrate, influence and put to good use
the growing intellect of the Oxford student body. Stansfeld challenged
students not to neglect their duty to their fellowman. The Stansfeld
Challenge was presented as more than just a challenge as Stansfeld
declared, it was their duty and he encouraged the students by inviting
them to the south side of town to see how the other side lived, and how
many were starving to death. Tubby responded to the good Doctor's
calling and followed him down to the London slum.

Upon his first arrival, Tubby was directed to where Doctor
Stansfeld was working. He stepped inside a room and behind a
partition Tubby was shocked by what he saw. There, sitting on a chair,
under a dim gaslight was a man in his fifties, James Weston, a man
who struggled to raise his children in respectable poverty, if there
could ever be such a thing. A grotesque bacterial growth covered his
entire face. The whole left side of the man's cheek had given way and
within the raw red cavity the inside of his mouth was visible. Never
before had Tubby seen such a sight and it terrified him.

Mr. Weston arrived every evening at the mission to have his wound
cleaned and dressed. The infection was so serious, unless it was
cleansed on a daily basis, it surely would have spread resulting in his

death. When Doctor Stansfeld looked up and saw Tubby's terrified reaction he asked Tubby to come closer and hold the basin while he carefully bathed the wound with small swabs. The young Tubby came forward, held the basin and immediately became immersed with helping out. All along, Doctor Stansfeld conversed with both Tubby and Mr. Weston in the most natural way, as if nothing was wrong. A young boy entered the room. Stansfeld was sensitive to the boy being unnerved by the sight of such a ghastly wound and turned in such a way as to block the boy's view of the open wound, and in doing so, in the most natural, unassuming manner, told Tubby, "Now we will change over. You take the syringe and cleanse the wound." Stansfeld then got up and attended to the young boy. The following evening Tubby was back again. When James Weston arrived, Doctor Stansfeld reminded Tubby, "You take the syringe, and I will hold the basin." By the end of the evening, Tubby learned the most important lesson in teaching social service: trust and transference.

Tubby learned the effective art of helping those in need not only rested in the art of giving but in the art of transferring, as it was then, one was able to intimately involve others. A critical lesson in social work, when executed in a relaxed and natural way, seamlessly perpetuated attending to the needs of others, while at the same time, involving the needed assistance of others. Tubby not only learned this important lesson from Doctor Stansfeld, who became famous for his work in London and India, he would put it to use in such a way he would "Hang his hat on it," so to speak, on what would become his one most inflexible rule: "Today's guest is tomorrow's host."

Upon graduation from Oxford, Tubby was invited to study theology under Reverend and Doctor Joseph Armitage Robinson, Dean of Westminster Abbey. It was a theological apprenticeship with hands on application. Back then, the theological college was a relatively new institution, the first having been founded in England towards the end of the nineteenth century. Tubby's apprenticeship was considered by many in the church to be controversial, whereas before, the tradition of studying religion at College was considered sufficient to complete one's course of study for life in the clergy. Later in life, when surrounded by the stuffiness of theological graduates, his fellow Brothers, Tubby stated, "Thank heaven, I was denied the privilege of a theological college."

Tubby was destined to the service of the Church. He took it to heart and wrote, "Not a servant, but a slave... a worker without contract, without any reward except by the grace and by kindness of his Master; a creature born to strict and humble obedience, devoid of any leisure belonging to himself; if idle, not dismissed, but scrapped as a sham tool. Dwell on this word, 'slave,' and awe comes back to you, the deepest need of our lives." Tubby was ordained into the Anglican Church–The Church of England–as a deacon in December 1910.

Portsea-Paris Church was one of the great parishes of the Church of England with a church body of fifty-six thousand! It was Tubby's first Anglican position and he joined the staff of eighteen clergymen as the most junior member. During the next five years, Tubby dedicated himself to the church, filling many positions. He learned he really loved people and he became adept at making many friends.

When the The Great War arrived the Vicar at Portsea sent four clergymen to the Western Front in the spring of 1915. Tubby was one of them and sent to Poperinge, Belgium, commonly known as "Pop," a small town of about 11,000 inhabitants. However, during peak operations of the war the population boomed to 250,000. Just eight miles from the front lines, Poperinge was located behind the most heavily fought for real estate on the Western Front and was vulnerable to German artillery. At times the shelling was heavy, but for the most part, intermittent and inaccurate, landing in streets, gardens and buildings with indiscretion. It was the last glimpse of civilization soldiers saw before marching into hell and the first they saw if they ever returned. The value of Poperinge for Tubby was its proximity to the front lines; it was directly accessible to the chief sufferers of the war.

When old men spoke of the mud and blood of Flanders that flowed for four years they were not exaggerating. Men stood for weeks up to their knees, even to their chests in water with their feet rotting, their guts and lungs collapsing. Mutilated companions would often lie all night besides their mates where the smell of rotting flesh was more fearsome than the threat of death itself, which in the end, no matter what one believed, was an escape from this living Hell.

Neville Talbot was the Senior Chaplain of the 6th Division stationed on the Ypres Salient. He was the son of the Bishop of Winchester who presided over a religious and prosperous family.

Neville was no stranger to Army life having been a chaplain to the 6th Division Rifle Brigade during the Boer War in South Africa. He stood tall at six feet seven inches and the spectacle of Neville riding on his seventeen and a half hands horse was inspiring.

During the autumn of 1914, Neville was ordered to remain behind the lines with a rear section of the Brigade Field Ambulance. Realizing he was needed in the thick of things, he disobeyed the standing order for chaplains not to minister to troops in the field during the heat of battle, an order known as the "Code of Confinement." Reverend Talbot strongly believed his place was with the men—His men— especially during their life and death struggle. Talbot joined the Sixth Infantry Division of the Third Battalion Rifle Brigade in battle, including many of the same soldiers he had been with in South Africa. By disobeying the Chaplain's Code, Reverend Talbot was admired and respected by the men and it was his deliberate action that changed Army regulations resulting with the Chaplain's Code being disregarded. After his action, all chaplains were free to accompany troops into the field of battle. During the war, more than one hundred Army Chaplains paid for that privilege with their lives. Neville Talbot and Tubby were already friends from back home and by special request it was arranged for Tubby to work under him. The two of them together were a sight to behold with Neville at six feet seven and Tubby at five feet two.

Tubby was a Christian in a hurry, in a hurry to speak to his fellow man. As a matter of fact, that was his sole purpose, to speak to his fellow man in such a way that they too caught his infection of urgency and would hurry about the Lord's work. He looked quite ordinary except for his piercing eyes behind his horn-rimmed glasses, eyes which looked deep into the souls of others.

Upon his arrival in Poperinge, Tubby moved around by horse, however he was nothing of a horseman and his horse sank to its belly in mud. He learned to travel by any means possible: by foot, army trucks, supply wagons, even by maneuvering a bike through the overcrowded streets which was a precarious affair. He greeted everyone from brass hats to privates with the same genuine enthusiasm. His infectious personality attracted attention and the realization grew throughout the Salient that Tubby was no ordinary chaplain.

Tubby had never experienced any real danger. He knew nothing of a soldier's agony, their living horrors. When confronted with the soldiers from the field; the men to a man, Tubby asked himself, "What could he say to any of them who would soon be returning to a living nightmare? How dare he say anything at all?" His words came slowly, haltingly, but were spoken with such open sincerity, men knew they were listening to the truth. When Tubby performed his first service on the Front Lines, he confessed he never felt more inarticulate or inadequate. Tubby learned there was only one thing he could speak of to the men in the trenches, the wounded, the fearful and the broken, and that was the truth of the Gospel.

Men were dying at the rate of 250 a day. Their needs were great. They needed friendship, the warmth of personal contact that could lift them above the daily horror of the battlefields and give them back a glimpse of sanity and civility. The Army decided there should be a Church House and a Club for the Sixth Division in Poperinge, close to the lines where soldiers could seek solace, if only briefly. The responsibility for locating such a house was commissioned to Neville Talbot who included Tubby in the task at hand. They learned of a house owned by a Mr. Coevoet Camerlynck just a few blocks from the town square. Camerlynck was a wealthy and ungenerous hop merchant who used his attic space to dry his hops. The back of the house had been struck by shrapnel, damaging the metal roof and bringing down much of the plaster ceiling. It shattered windows throughout the house, allowing a steady flow of wind and rain that caused further damage. After the blast, Coevoet was preparing to escape the dangers of Poperinge to the South of France, leaving his mansion located at 35 Rue de L'Hopital vacant.

Had the house been in good condition, it wouldn't have been available to the army. This was good fortune for Tubby and Reverend Talbot. In every sense of the word, although it was a small mansion, the house was a "fixer-upper" and Mr. Camerlynck was of no mind to make the necessary repairs only to have the house subjected to more damage. The Army offered to purchase the house, but the Belgium hop merchant would not sell. He was shrewd enough to know he might be able to command a higher price after the war and even if the house was destroyed, he would still own the land. He agreed to rent the house to the British Army, provided they made the needed repairs and maintained the house in first class condition. The rent was fixed at 150 francs per month and the house was destined to become one of the most famous houses of the war.

Once the house was secured, Reverend Talbot knew his stocky friend—a non-stop whirlwind of energy—was the perfect proprietor to run the house. And for Tubby this became the opportunity of a lifetime, this new Army Church House where Tubby learned, "It is only when each man acts like a brother that brotherhood can be truly achieved."

But what would they name the house? "Church House" was seriously pondered. General Reginald May insisted the house be named after Neville Talbot because of his heroic actions ending the Chaplains Code, but Neville strongly objected. Neville's younger brother, Gilbert had finished his studies at Oxford, and as one of the sons of the Bishop of Winchester, was a friend of the Prince of Wales. When the war arrived, he put aside his political ambitions and volunteered to serve his country. Convinced of the justice of the cause and the short duration of the war, he joined the Rifle Brigade, where his brother Neville was Senior Chaplain. Gilbert was immediately promoted to platoon commander and attached to the 7th Battalion. When he got his commission, the Colonel told him: "Don't forget you are responsible for 54 lives, not 55—yours doesn't count." Just before Gilbert ended his training, he wrote in his diary: "Whatever else is true of life, one thing is certain, that I am doing the right thing now and that every ounce in me must go to it till the end. The War is amazingly inspiring, and all the Belgian stories and all the devilish and damnable horrors that these swine inflict on women and children make one long to get there. And I still can't help reading the war news and the casualty lists without a sense of wondering whether someday my turn will come, and whether it is possible to imagine a finer thing happening to me." After nine months of training, his battalion crossed the Channel on May 19th, 1915.

When he experienced the Western Front, his thoughts about the war changed dramatically. Shocked by the destruction and the indescribable life in the trenches, he longed for home. There wasn't much left of his sparkling enthusiasm. Whenever he went through a difficult period, he tried to meet up with his brother or wrote a letter home. "I find it very hard only trying to describe what we have seen during our expedition. At times one's thoughts fly back to all the precious things in England, a thousand times more precious now. I think of Farnham, Winchester and Oxford in summer. And one thinks of all the family and the happy times we've had."

On July 30th, 1915, the Germans threw into battle another new weapon in this modern war. After the poison gas came the flame-thrower and it was used for the first time to get the 8th Battalion of the Rifle Brigade out of Hooge Crater. Gilbert was ordered to take part in the counterattack with his platoon. Private "Appy" Nash, Gilbert's orderly, describes the whole story: "The condition of the wood was unspeakable. Gilbert said: 'We're going up all together to a warm shop. I don't suppose many of us will come back.' We all waited from 2 to 2:40 while our side bombarded. Gilbert went up and down, cheering the men. He looked constantly at his watch. At 2:45 he blew the whistle which was the original signal to charge—and at once the men—only 16 were now available, leapt out, and rushed forward. Gilbert, followed closely by myself, headed them a few yards on, with the words: 'Come on my lads—this is our day.' Soon he came to the old British barbed wire fencing, which he was beginning to cut, when he was hit in the neck, and fell over the wire fencing."

Nash got shot five times while trying to save Gilbert. But the young officer could not be helped. When Nash managed to crawl back to the trenches, he immediately volunteered to go back with stretcher-bearers for his Lieutenant. More than one team tried to reach him, two even got as close as three meters. But the enemy fire was too dangerous. After some of the rescue party were shot, the Colonel ordered no more attempts could be made. Private Nash would later be awarded the Distinguished Conduct Medal for attending to a wounded officer under heavy enemy fire.

When Neville heard the terrible news, he was determined to get his brother out of No Man's Land. On August 1st, 1915 he wrote in his diary: "Just about dusk, I got into No-Man's Land, first found the body of young Woodroffe, and then found Gilbert's body. A terrible experience it was. I took his unit cap-badge out of his pocket. I stroked his hair and commended his soul to the Father, to the Son and to the Holy Spirit, and prayed that we might meet again. There was nothing more that I could do that night, so I got back into the trench."

A week later he had another try and wrote in his diary: "August 7th. Hearing that the attack was put off for 24 hours, my resolution hardened to go up again and carry through the burial. How strong is the sense of outrage at non-burial in one's blood! In the trench was a post of East-Yorkshires—angels they were, for I no sooner said what I was about than one man had hopped out, and another had got hold of a stretcher, and, after I had run out (doubled up) to verify what one man had said, that a light-haired body was still there, a group sprang out and the poor body was carried in."

After plunging through the muddy labyrinth of duckboards (wooden walkways in the trenches) for a few miles, they reached Gilbert's final resting place: Sanctuary Wood Cemetery. A Royal Engineer made him a wooden cross and carved "Word of Peace" on it. Since the cemetery was located only a few yards away from the front line, the cross on Talbot's grave was blown to pieces at least two times. Each time his devoted brother made sure a new grave marker was put up. After the Armistice, Neville had an oak cross made. It read: "Fear not, I am He that liveth and was dead, and behold I am alive evermore."

While Reverend Talbot would have nothing to do with the house being named after him, he agreed the House could be named "Talbot House" in honor of his youngest brother. When the initials of Talbot House where translated into the Army Signalers Code for calling letters by symbolic syllables, "Talbot House" translated into "Toc H." Troops often spoke in code and instead of saying "Let's go down to Talbot House in Poperinge," they'd say, "Let's go down to Toc H in Pop." In time, throughout all of Flanders, the house became known as Toc H. A hostel in a town full of troops where Tubby infected a small Belgium mansion with an atmosphere of purpose that gave to each man, of every class and rank, a hint of the qualities that had the texture of eternity.

As far as the impossible position held by the British and the Allies known as the Ypres Salient, Tubby wrote: "What was it in the victim Belgium which refused to own defeat in the first hopeless winter? It is that quality which needs a name. I know of no description of this virtue to be compared with that in the New Testament: 'Blessed are those which have not seen and yet have believed.' To call it fortitude, to call it pluck, to call it courage, patience, perseverance, misses its source–a faith in human destiny, a dogged certainty that right must triumph. This dogged certainty surely descended in power from God upon a line so thin, so worn, so harassed, without reinforcements, that an attack brought sanitary orderlies and company cooks into the Line not once but on so many occasions... I recall and always shall recall, the reinforcements which we then received: the 1918 class, boys straight from school, who filled old Talbot House for a few days with their fresh laughter and with their undimmed purpose. Most of these boys, many the youngest sons were swept into the tide of war which followed, and died too soon to taste its bitterness."

With the help of many volunteers and donations the house was repaired. For Tubby, the most important job was to make the house feel like a real home—a home away from home. The new Innkeeper was determined to create a place where men could relax in comfort and for a few hours or days, forget the war. Ladies back home learned about the needs of the house and soon crates of furniture, pots and pans, curtains, rugs, framed pictures, along with boxes of books, tablecloths, wastepaper baskets, clocks and flower vases were sent to Talbot House. Maps of Britain and pictures of the countryside were hung on the walls. Nothing was placed in the house to remind anybody of the war. A piano was donated and from then on, all the songs sung could be accompanied with a keyboard.

On the ground floor there was a large entrance hall, flanked by a decorative drawing room, a rest room and a dining room converted into a recreation room with a refreshment bar. There was a ground floor office, kitchen and a staircase leading to the upper floors. Upstairs on the first floor (in the U.S. this would be the second floor as the English call the first floor the ground floor) was a large landing, three bedrooms, a large nursery on the balcony and the Chaplain's (Tubby's) office. There was a writing room and a library, the most remarkable on the Western Front with more than 2,000 books. To borrow a book, the soldier left his cap and if the book was more valuable than the cap, well then... On the second floor (in the states the third floor) the bedrooms were communal with stretcher beds and blankets to be used to accommodate soldiers and officers for a night or two. Above everything stood the attic–a great hop loft–covering the entire house, reached, not by a staircase but by a steep ladder that had to be carefully climbed.

It was a proper house, a home—a soldier's home. Nothing was under lock and key, the house belonged to any and all who were present, and it relied upon the occupants to be kind to her, pickup after her, repair her and maintain her. There were vases full of cut flowers, easy chairs for rest and relaxation, an open fireplace, even a house cat. A cup of tea, a good book, a cot to rest upon, a billiard table, an ongoing discussion, a debate even, a meal, a sing-a-long, a joke, a hearty "Hello" or "Look who's here!" There were plays and in time, Talbot House had its own eleven-piece orchestra. It was a place to welcome guests and it was a place to be welcomed. Identities were restored, personalities came back to life and for a moment—a day or two—the war was forgotten. It was a place to feel warm, restored and valued as if you were somebody, and that somebody actually cared about you.

Tubby implemented his one standing and inflexible rule, the one he learned from Doctor Stansfeld: the art of helping those in need not only rested in the art of giving but in the art of transference. A large sign was posted in the house for all to read: "Today's Guest Is Tomorrow's Host." The troops were reminded, quite definitively, what had been done for them today, they were expected to do for the men that came tomorrow. It was how the continuity and unique atmosphere of Talbot House operated.

It is wonderful how a childlike spirit appeals to men, it seems to have the power of drawing out the very best in them. It was said of Tubby, he was the one man who could make men forget the artificial and temporary distinctions of rank, and have men "meet upon the higher ground of their common manhood." He had a way of making shy souls feel decently important. Tubby never thought about rank or the status that commonly separates men. Things of that nature would only get in his way and simply did not exist for the impetuous Tubby. At Talbot House, one never knew whether you were rubbing shoulders with a General or a "Tommy" and it was not unusual to find an officer tidying up the ashtrays or sweeping the floors. There were no airs about it, the influence of Tubby Clayton presided over the entire house where the rigid hierarchy of the Army was just not allowed as evident by the prominently displayed signs posted throughout the house which read: "IF YOU ARE IN THE HABIT OF SPITTING ON THE CARPET AT HOME, PLEASE SPIT HERE," or "COME INTO THE

GARDEN AND FORGET ABOUT THE WAR" and "THIS IS A
LIBRARY, NOT A DORMITORY" and "THE WASTE-PAPER
BASKETS ARE PURELY ORNAMENTAL." Then there was the
infamous sign with a hand pointing the way, "TO PESSIMISTS, WAY
OUT ☞ " and over the door of Tubby's office a legend of a sign:
"ALL RANK ABANDON YE WHO ENTER HERE."

Tubby wasted no time in turning Talbot House into a pub of the
highest social order, an Episcopalian saloon, what the Canadians
called a "soft drink" establishment, meaning no alcohol was allowed.
Yet no one resented lapping up a good cup of hot cocoa or tea. It was
not an Officer's Club, nor was it a club for the "Rank and File." It was
as the signboard outside proudly proclaimed and which hangs there to
this day, "Everyman's Club."

When entering the recreation hall, one directed their attention to the
Notice Board where announcements and the rules of the House were
posted daily by the hand of the Innkeeper Jester. These announcements
were well worth studying because of their profound absurdities along
with the continuously changing busy scheduled of weekly activities.
Each announcement was clever and lost nothing in the telling. At a
time when humor was needed, Tubby's weekly good-natured chivalry
was popular and welcomed. All notices were friendly, humorous and
not in the least bit institutional such as: "THE GOOD PLAYER
CHALKS HIS CUE BEFORE HE PLAYS; THE BAD PLAYER
AFTERWARDS" or with misspellings such as "NO SWARING
ALOUD HEAR!"

The House didn't start with a stated purpose, it started with a
person: Tubby Clayton who instilled the experience that Talbot House
was a sanctuary for everyman. From its earliest days, Talbot House
was evolving into something more significant than just an Army club
and a Church House, it was acquiring the strength of a simple
philosophy capable of radiating the noblest of thoughts and desires of
men. It knew the part God meant for it to perform towards the
thousands of men who came in, wave after wave from the lowly plains
of Flanders. It spoke to them of home, relationships, of love, of duty
and it breathed the courage of Christ upon them. Here they laid down
their grief, their fears, their burdens and the relentless pain of war, and
they emerged comforted and renewed. Tubby summed up the meaning

of the House when he said, "If you sow clubs you reap clubs, but if you sow the kingdom of God you reap the kingdom of God."

On pushing through the door one visitor wrote, "I found myself at once in a different world. It was amazing. I felt like Alice when she stepped through the looking-glass. There were soldiers all round me, of course, and Army slang in the air, but, in stepping across the threshold, I seemed to have left behind me all the depression and wariness of the street."

Tubby maintained the House with an uninterrupted schedule of daily church services, concerts, debates, card games, chaplains' conferences and all the while, with songs, meals and tea. Tubby was blessed with a unique metabolism that often allowed him to limit his sleeping to just three hours per night. He was always in a hurry; for him there was just so much to do, and he was perpetually running late, panting behind each appointment. His tremendous sense of urgency bound him to an impossible timetable, born of his conviction that the war was not really one of shells and bayonets, but entirely a question of character. Accepting the hideous realities of war, what remained to be seen in the outcome was whether the character of the Allies was nearer to God than that of the fellows on the other side, and it was the job of the Good Padre to see that it was. He performed his self-imposed duties without the slightest trace of bitterness, remaining incredibly cheerful throughout it all and wrote: "Each week of course brings its deeper work–interviews, confessions, and other opportunities of which I am not worthy. It's a happy life, isn't it?"

One of the strange realities of the house: you never knew who you would see again, or if you yourself would ever make it back from the Front. There was a focused energy on one's time in the house, realizing this could be your last, and you might as well make the best of it while in such good company. Those were memorable times with death lurking around the corner. Here, the laughter of men was momentarily freed from fear by a jolly priest who had learned the secret of losing his own fears was in serving the needs of others. Soldiers knew and feared they could face certain death in their next mission, yet at Talbot House, they received the best protection of all and were prepared for battle as Tubby fitted them with their helmet of faith.

As for humor, Tubby learned the heartache of loss was unspoken and laughter was the wholesome antidote that could heal open wounds. Tubby's humor was clean and good fun, much of which had been lost or forgotten in the trenches, where in so many instances, humor had to be dirty or degrading to be funny. In true humor, this is not the case and men must have good humor to feel alive. It's been said troops will go an additional mile under the inspiration of a good joke.

For Tubby, clothing was nothing but a necessary chore which he never had the time to get quite right, his buttons were coming off, his pants were overly worn with holes at the knees and his shirt cuffs were tattered. The typical image of Tubby was a short and round, unassuming, shabbily dressed man, wrapped in an oversized coat with horn-rimmed glasses. Such a sight bestowed a deceptive air of innocence when he arrived at some remote entrenched position along the Front, announcing to the Commander there would be an extra guest that night. Within moments, he'd have the place in laughter and even the proximity of shell-fire could do little to restrain the infectious enthusiasm that just arrived. His "slumming," as Tubby would refer to it became a moving fixture on Salient life, and a visit from Tubby did more for the morale of the troops than any pep talk from a Commanding Officer.

Tubby and the House needed a Chapel. After the House had been divided up, there was nothing left – except the attic. In a hop house the attic is where hops are dried prior to brewing the yeast to still the beer. Tubby had a different plan in mind for his attic space which would involve a fermentation of a different kind, the fermentation of the spirit. "On the first day of the Feast of Unleavened Bread, when it was customary to sacrifice the Passover lamb, Jesus' disciples asked him, 'Where do you want us to go and make preparations for you to eat the Passover?' So He sent two of His disciples telling them 'Go into the city, and a man carrying a jar of water will meet you. Follow him. Say to the owner of the house he enters, 'The Teacher asks: Where is my guest room, where I may eat the Passover with my disciples?' He will show you a larger upper room, furnished and ready. Make preparations for us there." - Gospel of Mark.

It was in the Upper Room where Jesus celebrated the Last Supper with his Disciples and said, "A new commandment I give you: Love one another. As I have loved you, so you must love one another. By this all men will know that you are my disciples, if you love one another... My command is this: Love each other as I have loved you. Greater love has no one than this that he lay down his life for his friends." And Jesus proclaimed, "I am the way, the truth, and the life: no one comes to the Father except through me." It was there in the Upper Room where Jesus performed the first communion, where he broke the bread and said, "This is my body, which is broken for you; do this in remembrance of me" and he took the cup saying, "This cup is the new covenant in my blood; do this, whenever you drink it, in remembrance of me."

The final floor: the attic, became the heart and soul of Talbot House—the Chapel—or as Tubby appropriately named it, "The Upper Room." To enter the Chapel, everyone would have to climb carefully, arm over arm, step by step to make the journey to the House's spiritual sanctuary. Regarding this upward climb Tubby wrote, "There are no further stairs; but a ladder. Stairways represent a certain ease which should exist between the movement of man and men; but no one can be easy towards their movement towards God."

To Tubby's delight, an old carpenter's bench was found in the garden shed which would serve as the altar. It reminded Tubby of the humble beginnings of Jesus, a carpenter's apprentice who tooled, shaped and transformed the wood. The large bench was lugged to the Upper Room where it became the altar for all the services and where it stands to this day.

Of the house Tubby wrote: "'Begin on the Ground Floor with Everyman,' murmurs old Talbot House, 'that is the first step. Welcome him, amuse him, surprise him and excite his interest. Help him to find out where his friends are stationed. Confidence means falling in together, help this to happen. I have got to turn these strangers into friends. I have got to get these visitors concerned. I must think out each step. I must study my customers as they move from the threshold inwards. Here is a Notice Board to win a smile. Yonder is a map where they can find their homes. I must not be distressed,' said the Old House, 'if any men come in and get no further than the ground floor. This does not mean I've failed. Help me to recognize, Eternal Master, that your method is the truest courtesy. You do not wish us to force men upstairs. If they can be persuaded, well and good; but we will have no force used in your house beyond the influence exercised by love.'"

Tubby considered Easter Sunday in 1916 to be the happiest of his ministry where he single handedly conducted ten Easter celebrations from 5:00 a.m. until noon in the Upper Room. The Front Line had been fiercely engaged and Tubby hoped by having a succession of services, many of the men would be able to get in at odd times during the morning. Every service was packed, while the floor below the chapel was filled with men waiting to replace those already above. All Tubby could do for seven hours straight was to Lift, Break Bread and Give. On that day of worship and historical redemption, Tubby recalled it was God's voice who spoke to all who were present, comforting them with: "It is I: be not afraid."

After morning services, Tubby headed out into the field to perform more services. When he returned to the Old House that evening he found it packed to the gills. He departed again at 8:30 p.m. as one of the orderlies of the House had been wounded and was asking for him at Number 17 Casualty Clearing Station. Duty called, and he set off once again, not knowing exactly where the hospital was. He left his car, took off on foot, cut across the landscape and crawled under a train. He emerged oily and breathless, found the tented casualty station and his dear friend. He arrived back at the House near midnight, ready for supper. It had been quite a full day—joyful, challenging and exhausting.

By the spring of 1917 the staff of the house reached seventeen and almost everyone who fought on the Salient made their way, sooner or later, to Talbot House. And once having passed through the front door, there were very few who did not find their way to the Upper Room. Tubby held services and gave communion to the men wearing the uniforms of a dozen nations, some who were just mere boys. Tubby was prepared for them and said, "No inanimate memorial can compare in the sight of God with a living witness, trained and equipped, and eager for his share in the task of reconciliation both of man with God and of man with man."

Many times, the Upper Room was filled with hundreds of men engaged in song and prayer while the town was being bombarded. Men were baptized by Tubby and received their first communion and for all too many, it was their last. When men live surrounded by violence the actions of ordinary living are blown away and the presence of the Almighty can feel "Oh so near," beckoning and calling. With the opportunity looming above, many journeyed to the Upper Room, and within the sanctuary of Talbot House, hearts were restored, identities identified.

The best description of the Upper Room was penned by Tubby in a poem:

THE CHAPEL
Here is a quiet room!
Pause for a little space;
And in the deepening gloom
With hands before thy face,
Pray for God's grace.

Let no unholy thought
Enter thy musing mind;
Things that the world has wrought–
Unclean–untrue–unkind–
Leave these behind.

Pray for the strength of God,
Strength to obey His plan;
Rise from your knees,
More of a man
Than when your prayer began.

Man can follow his own philosophy to a certain point under the most surprising and difficult of circumstances, however, sooner or later, such understanding and strength is doomed to failure and will fall. The Upper Room was not just a quiet, peaceful room. Here there was the Mountain of Transfiguration where men came with fear and discovered courage; where men came out of the darkness and were given light; where men came broken and found the One who had the will to be broken for them, and in that, their souls rejoiced.

Men of the noblest spirit regarded worship in the Upper Room as preparation for their dangerous duties. Cynics could argue men came on selfish grounds; to plead for self-preservation—and could anyone blame them if they did? Tubby said, "I can testify that for the most part the urgency with them was not fear. Here is a scrap in evidence of this, a penciled intercession written by an unknown man for use in the Upper Room after he himself had gone up to the Line. Its date is 29/3/17, and I have no clue whatever to his identity. Out of the past, therefore, speaks this unknown voice from a man asking for prayer. He does not, as one might expect, ask prayers for his own safety, still less for comfort. He does the two things that Our Lord loves: he asks to be helped and to help others, and he speaks of himself humbly as having traveled far from God. Here, then, is the request of the Unknown Soldier: 'Will you pray very earnestly for me that I may have strength given me to do that which is right and to make an effort to help others; not so much by what I say, but by my whole life. I have wandered away very far, but I want to put things right; and the prayers of Talbot House will mean much to me.'"

There has been a great deal of discussion over the years about "foxhole religion" and no doubt, the First World War had its share of "shell-fire converts." The men who came to the Upper Room were sincerely anxious to reconcile what faith they had, or were about to receive. To many, their brief time in the Chapel was their prelude to eternity. To others, it was the beginning of a new life that would carry them over into peacetime. The cynics and the slackers seldom got beyond the billiard room; it was the sensitive, the curious and those who were completely broken from the inside out who found their way upstairs.

Tubby wrote: "Old Talbot House was no confused conception. It knew the part God meant it to perform towards the multitudes of homeless men, wave after wave in the low Flanders plains. It spoke to them of Home, of love, of duty. It breathed the courage of Christ upon them. Here they laid up their grief, their fears, and their burdens. Hence, they emerged, comforted and renewed. What they found there depended on themselves, for every guest of the half million soldiers who came to Talbot House was free to choose. No orders went the rounds. No martial mandates moved man to climb to the old Upper room. A hint dropped here and there in conversation, a sense of curiosity, a friend's example, or a long-latent aspiration to follow more nearly, kept the old hop-loft rarely undermanned."

The whole house breathed happiness and anyone who entered it was better for it. It was not the only Church House or club on the Western Front—far from it, but it was the most unique and it possessed some indefinable quality of radiance other army houses were unable to attain. And "Why" it was asked? "Why was it so popular with the men?" The answer was really quite simple. There was only one Tubby Clayton and the glowing intimate atmosphere of the House was the actual projection of the wit, laughter and the friendliness of the man himself.

Soldiers know how the horrors of war can devastate a man. It is incomprehensible to eyes that have not seen, to ears that have not heard, to the heart that has not pounded to the surrounding terror to understand what a soldier goes through. And Tubby was there, on the battlefield, in the trenches and at Talbot House. "No eyes," he wrote, "which have looked upon these things in actuality can ever hope to find their like in any church on earth. The intense reality, the humble eagerness, the unity of aim, the thought of one another, the constancy of friendship thus forever knit, were like great shafts of light streaming upon a dark and narrow way, where on a Figure all—commanding stood plainly to be seen. The crouching men, outlined in candlelight against the background of oozing boards upon the yielding carpet of moist clay (the trenches) made this the Food of Immortality indeed, delivered within the sepulcher itself. Death stood without and knocked, but Christ within forbade his instant entry; for, even as we knelt, such sounds came very near."

Although he tried to be the last to show it, Tubby said his heart was either in his mouth or in his boots while visiting and holding services for the troops in the trenches along the Front. He did not relish the danger but was not afraid of it and he showed the soldiers that death is far from the worst thing that can happen to a man. Tubby was brave because he was afraid; afraid for every man out there. He was courageous because he heard God's calling and he answered it by rising above his own personal fears, the bombs blasting, the gas mixing with the air and the bullets whizzing by. He answered God's calling by serving all who were around him and in doing so, he delivered himself to God through service towards others.

When he realized the gravity of the situation around him he struggled. Men were facing death daily. Men were coughing out their lungs from the gas and drowning in the mud. In such deprivation, Tubby witnessed the absence of faith and saw a moratorium on Christianity. He knew all the illusions and innocent excitement regarding the "Glory" of war were gone. These men knew they were in Hell and held out with only one hope—to go home. Tubby knew he would have to muster all the humor, courage and intelligence God had endowed him with, if he were, in any way, going to be of any use or good.

In recognizing the shear madness of his surrounding circumstances, Tubby wrote, "If the world will go mad, it must expect to suffer. The whole business sometimes seems sheer insanity on a huge scale." Then there was the quote from an unknown soldier which pretty much summed everything up: "Well, if we're winning this bloody war, God'elp the losers."

It wasn't as if Tubby didn't have his bad days or was the perfect human being, he wasn't. His personal constitution drove him to occupy every waking minute of every day with the activities of his faith. It is impossible for anyone to keep such a schedule and it did catch up with Tubby. At times, he was deathly sick for days, weeks and months, and on more than one occasion, his temperature rose to one hundred and five and a guard was posted at his bedroom door to keep visitors away. At times, he was intolerable and so steadfast in his determination he didn't pay attention to the bureaucracy of rules surrounding the war, such as keeping the proper accounting records for the maintenance and care of the House. There were those who were frustrated by his often-complete disregard for regulations, military protocol and lack of decorum, along with being agitated by his nerve racking persistence once he set his mind to something. Tubby had no concept of the management of time, space or money. Tubby regarded time as purely an arbitrary division of the day, space was something better ignored, and money was something he didn't relate to. He was perpetually running late, although his theory on this was, "The only way to arrive in time is to start out late." It was surprising he typically only ran thirty minutes behind schedule. His work never ended, and he refused to take to the meaning of the word "No." However, as irritated as one could get with the man, one always had to appreciate his accomplishments and the direction of the wind that blew Tubby forward.

Such was Tubby's life and routine, if there was anything that could be considered routine about it. He kept going for years: Talbot House, the front lines, behind the lines, services, funerals, letters to loved ones, visits to supply depots, and observation posts. Wherever the men were he was there for them. Tubby described his situation, "To live day after day not only in danger but in squalor; to be gypsies in season and out, in a nightmare fit for Cain; to be homeless amid   all that is hideous and disheartening, habituated only to a foreground of filth and to a horizon of apparently invincible menace; to move always among the wreckage of men's lives and hopes, haunted not only by a sense of being yourself doomed to die, but by an agony of mind which cried out at every step against the futile folly of the waste of time and of treasure, of skill and of life itself—this is what war meant to a soul sensitive to such impressions."

The house experienced an intense amount of foot traffic with shocks from daily bombardments shaking its foundation. There were concerns about the structural integrity of the old house, especially in the Upper Room which was not designed to hold the weight of hundreds of men. There were no upright structural posts to support the center beam, just a long open space supported from the sides. There were rumors, word of the House had gotten back to the Germans and they were zeroing in on it. With so many attending, it would have been a huge blow to morale for the House to have been destroyed. Chaplain Harold Bates had his leg shattered when a bomb exploded in the street as he left the House. Two brothers were wounded when they approached the front door and the restaurant directly across the street was obliterated. A bomb landed in the garden, the concert hall platform collapsed and water pipes were ruptured. Yet, Tubby would have no part of any discussion to relocate the House to a safer environment. He wanted to remain as close as possible to the needs of its occupants. One summer afternoon in 1917, a large naval shell blew the house next door to ashes, causing Talbot House to shudder. The seven hundred men crowded into the house and garden, were stunned into silence. When Tubby rushed about expecting to find blood and casualties he came across only one victim—a soldier who had been relaxing in an easy chair, sharpening his pencil with a pocket knife who cut his finger. Other than minor shell damage, the old house was never put out of commission and rocked and rolled its way through the war with very little damage.

Tubby refused to be confined, whether within the walls of Talbot House or throughout the Salient. His spirit was a presence, bringing comfort, laughter, fellowship and in that nightmare of Hell, the continuous unfolding spirit of God. He followed his men to wherever they were. He shared in their dangers and understood by the grace of God, he was there for them and ultimately, when the opportunity arose—and there were many—he would be in a position to point them to the Almighty. Whether out in the field in the thick of battle, or at some bored sentry post, Tubby made his rounds, arriving to lead men in prayer and bring them communion. On any given day, Tubby might be leading a hilarious sing-a-long in a battery outpost under fire, burying the disfigured body of a young boy or writing a letter to his parents. It didn't matter where he was or where he was going, what mattered is wherever he went, he carried with him the spirit of Christ.

Tubby learned to speak spontaneously and passionately for hours on end, in a manner that pinged-ponged between the sublime and good humor, on any subject matter which was as inspiring as it was entertaining. He spoke to the men in the trenches, the field hospitals, artillery posts, supply posts and sentry posts. He spoke to them from the actual environment of their suffering. When he spoke, it wasn't from a pulpit or from any church hierarchy; it was from the heart. He learned to never doubt those he had been commissioned to serve and to automatically just trust them, saying, "All his geese were swans."

Trust: one of the most difficult things to achieve and one so easily deceived and violated. Trust of one's self—if one ever can—then trust in others, which is littered with a minefield of betrayals. Tubby learned to set himself apart from that so easily broken. "No, these men deserved better than that." Tubby would have nothing to do with such a vulnerable trust, he had no time for it or its consequences and he humbled himself to complete trust in the Lord. Tubby took it one giant step forward, if he was to truly trust in the Lord, then who was he to stand in the way of God by distrusting others. No, he absolutely, positively would not do that. As a matter of relationship, he would always take the first step and put his trust on "Auto Pilot—God Pilot" and trust his fellowman. Tubby would later say, "Suspect a man, and he will soon merit your suspicion. Distrust your team, and the team will melt away."

It is here, in the mystery of such a wasteful conflict where we can endeavor to understand life as it teeters back and forth on the tightrope of life and death, bringing many soldiers to their knees when they realized that only with the hope and faith in Christ can they conquer death. Whatever the weather, which was desperately foul at times, however heavy the shell-fire or gas attacks were, Tubby made his rounds, accompanied in the field with his Communion case, which he commonly referred to as the "Crown Jewels."

One morning, Tubby was making his rounds with one of his aides in a field towards Ypres. They took shelter in an old farm house and surveyed the muddy field ahead under bombardment. Tubby's destination was a group of soldiers manning the outermost trenches of the Front. They assessed their chances of making it across the field where the mud was as much the enemy as opposing snipers. The air was filled with smoke and the field pitted with craters. The bombardment slowed. Tubby decided they'd make a dash for it and they zigzagged past the shell holes and across the exploding field. Upon arrival, breathless and splattered in mud, they were led to a large tunnel where many of the men had gathered. When they entered, the shelling started up again, including the gas. A thick curtain was dropped behind them, sealing them in the cave.

Tubby held a service, blessed the host and gave communion. When they moved to depart, the curtain would not give way. The men pushed on it and it fell aside, revealing the dead body of a young soldier who had fallen against it. He was about eighteen and so gently had death touched him, he appeared to be asleep. He was well known to all and represented the beauty of youth being sacrificed so easily and innocently. Only two weeks prior, Tubby had welcomed him to Talbot House where he received his first and last communion. He was manning the furthest most guns and remained behind to protect the rear. He followed after his mates, hoping to be in time for Communion. But just before he could enter, while his mates received communion, he died. They placed his body to the side, so the other men might not see his innocent face as they left the cave.

After all had departed, Tubby inquired to the officer in charge if there were any who didn't have the opportunity to receive

Communion. The officer told Tubby there were five forward signalers who were unable to leave their posts, stationed fifty yards ahead on the embankment being heavily shelled. Tubby made his way through the bombardment to where the soldiers were crouching on the side of a slope. They all moved to higher ground and kneeled in the act of contrition, while death screamed above them. Tubby proceeded to minister to them, prayed for them and just as he was about to release the latch on his Communion case, a huge shell exploded just fifteen feet away, scattering jagged steel with a deathly whine. The men had all humbly removed their helmets and knelt there unprotected, but not one of them was touched. It might be said, not one of them was frightened. For within that moment of acute danger and death, they knew Christ was with them. Completely oblivious to all but the task at hand, Tubby recited the Lord's Prayer, rose and gave the blessing and ministered Communion. Afterwards, he stumbled down the embankment and away from the Field of Honor.

The Germans were making their big push to overtake Ypres and the surrounding area, including Poperinge. Commander Douglas Haig said, "Our backs are to the wall." The town was evacuated, and Talbot House was ordered to close. At first, Tubby remained steadfast, refusing to close the House and continuing to offer service to those troops moving through the deserted town. On May 21st, imperative orders came through, "The House must close." Tubby made his last entry into the House journal, "The authorities are determined that the House should be evacuated now. For a fortnight it has been the only House open in the town; and as the town is now altogether out of bounds, it seems only folly to remain," with his final words: "We have been wonderfully guarded and blessed; and though many of our children are now at peace, there are still many in this world who have here found Him and been found of Him - Much Love-Tubby."

After the House closed, locals who remained behind entered the House. They collected, removed and hid most of the furniture and objects, protecting them from the Germans who swept into the surrounding area and re-commissioned the house for their use. Immediately, upon the German retreat, the locals rushed back in and retook possession of the historic house.

The house reopened on September 27, 1918 at the commencement of the Fourth and final Battle of Ypres. This time, the Allies were

commanded and led by King Albert I of Belgium and swept the
Germans from the Ypres Salient in just twenty-four hours. From then
on, the rapid advances of the Allies left the house "high and dry." A
few detachments dropped in now and then, however the troops were
anxious not to linger as they were infected with the fever of pending
Victory. This was the end, and after four long years, men were in no
mood to stand about however inspiring the company. To those who
remained long enough, they were able to hear Tubby's final words in
the Upper Room. He spoke of death and destruction and denied they
were identical. He spoke of those who had gone before and of those
who remained and concluded by saying: "So tonight, here in this old
Chapel, the Spiritual center for three years of the Salient now finally
freed, between us and those who have freed it there lies that great belt
of desolation we know only too well. It is hideous still, but full of fear
no longer; for those who have at last broken the ring of death are far
beyond it now: out of sight, because victorious; vanished, because
advancing. Desolation, it is true, divides us but neither we nor they are
desolate. We go on our way here for the time, happy for the
knowledge that their feet, as they go forward, are on ever firmer
ground."

In all, half a million soldiers were guests at the house during the
war. They came from all over: Great Britain, Australia, New Zealand,
Canada, India, Belgium, South Africa, Scotland, and in the end,
America. After the war ended, the house was returned back to its
owner.

In 1919, Reverend Neville Talbot wrote: "…the laughter, the
friendship and the love which radiated from his great heart into the
wilderness of war round Ypres and 'Pop.' As I claim no credit for the
House and but gladly attribute it to one to whom, under God, it is due,
I can say that I think Talbot House was the ideal Church Institute.
Though it was 'dry,' it suggests a future for all Christian public-houses
to be open to all the world, full of friendship, hominess, fun, music,
games, laughter, books, pictures and discussion. And at the top, in the
loft, obtruding upon no one, but dominating everything, was the
Chapel–a veritable shrine, glowing with the beauty of holiness. Thus
above and below, the House was full of the Glory of God."

Chapter Three

Toc H

"Toc H owed its birth to the very special gifts of the Reverend Philip Clayton. Over the years it has attempted to heal the divisions in society, not through grand schemes but in the simplest yet most effective way, by creating friendships between individuals. Many thousands of people have been inspired by Toc H to express their faith by giving practical help to those in need. In today's society the movement is as necessary as it was in the very different world of the 1920s and 1930s." Queen Elizabeth

The end of the First World War brought about the temporary relief of a horrific conflict. What remained was Germany's discontent with their worldly position along with their anger towards those in their society they considered to be impure: the Jews, the mentally and physically handicapped, homosexuals and the Gypsies. The worldly tension accompanied by the death and destruction of so many innocents would take a twenty-year hiatus. The pursuit of pleasure arrived and for those who were ready and could afford it, they'd kick up their heels, cut loose and throw themselves a party. In the states it was known as the "Roaring Twenties" and in Europe the "Golden Twenties." But for the disenfranchised, the times were uneasy, and a further danger arose. After the euphoric glow of peace quickly faded, reality set in and there the world stood, bleak and bewildered. Soup lines, homelessness, poverty and unemployment infected the United Kingdom and wartime heroes roamed the streets looking for work. A new battle line entrenched itself: the war on poverty, desolation and unemployment.

For Tubby, the popular craze for "a good time" threatened the very tenants of his faith. Whereas the war years demanded a common service to achieve victory and from that shared experience real fellowship blossomed. Tubby realized peace brought a greater challenge and service towards others would have to take on a new meaning. From the fellowship experienced at Talbot House, developed and promoted by the good Padre, there was the camaraderie of hope. After the war, Tubby continued to believe in those relationships embodied and embolden in the Upper Room and he dreamed those friendships could carry over into the challenges facing postwar England.

Tubby was always exhilarated at the continuing discovery of himself when he met and discovered new people. He knew his most abiding love, founded in his faith in God was for his fellow-man. For the men who knew Tubby, they had the confidence Tubby knew them personally, recognized them as unique individuals, trusted and valued them. Simply put, Tubby's friendship with men was the halfway-house to their relationship with God.

Tubby lived through times of complete devastation, death and tragedy. He understood how the human spirit could prevail with God's influence. Once again, Tubby endeavored to move forward, and before he knew it, the momentum from those memories, experiences and relationships would carry him into the next exciting chapter of his life: the rebuilding of postwar England, and with that, to almost every corner of the earth.

He knew it wasn't necessary for him to convince men of anything, there would be another power attending to that. All he could do was call his brothers, let them know the camaraderie of Talbot House was calling them back to the noble action of service. He hoped and prayed the guests of Talbot House would answer that calling. What Tubby didn't know, was to what extent this call would be answered.

He had no plan or idea of inaugurating a Movement. What was to happen throughout the world was an unforeseen consequence originating from the exceptional and brave faith of one man, transcended through thousands of soldiers who fought on the Ypres Salient. Tubby would not glorify the war or promote a self-serving reminiscent group, an exclusive fraternity of wartime stories and memories. What he desired was to capture the very spirit of those men from Talbot House and to pass it on to a peacetime society; to do what he did before and address the needs of all around him. Tubby realized, "Peace brought an even greater challenge than war and that 'service' took on a new and incalculable meaning. If men wished to live in a sane and improving world then each must recognize the responsibility to their fellow man."

To begin again, Tubby needed a name. What to call this new—whatever it was to be—post war group of volunteers? What seemed natural was to use the existing name: Talbot House. However, Reverend Neville Talbot's father was a well-known respected Bishop in the Church of England and had already put the name "Talbot" to many uses. Any further use of the name would only cause confusion. Yet, it was important to bond the name of Talbot House to what Tubby was doing. It was decided to call it "Toc H," a very odd name for a new society of service. There were many who said it would never catch on. But catch on it did, with the advantage of being familiar to ex-servicemen, arousing in them their fondest memories of what had been the most difficult time in their lives, along with it being thought provoking to strangers; "Just what is this Toc H anyway?"

Governmental agencies had long been burdened with bureaucracy which often lost the genuineness of helping others through a regimented, impersonal approach. Tubby dreamt of a new touch to social service, replacing the chilly detachment of the established institutionalized approach. He wanted to see the rewards of giving were not isolated to just the recipient, but transposed to the character of the giver, as Jesus proclaimed, "It is more blessed to give than to receive."

The idea was first discussed during the war in 1917 when Tubby and a few intimates had the vision to transplant the camaraderie of Talbot House to a club in London, where the tradition of friendship, forged in the furnace of the Salient could continue. Once that seed had been planted in Tubby, it would never leave. In 1918, Tubby sent out more than 2,000 Christmas cards to the men whose names and

addresses were kept on the guest book at Talbot House and in
September of 1919, Tubby's book, *Tales of Talbot House* was
published.

The world continued to spin round and round with more inventions
and industrial advancements. There were changes in the economy and
society and the emergence of a middle-class, yet nothing had really
changed when it came to the needs of the human spirit. At first,
Tubby's idea had little shape or direction, just his desire to pursue two
noble causes. First was "Camaraderie;" the spirit of fellowship towards
one another. The second was "Service;" the idea of giving their very
best, without thought or reward, to a cause greater than themselves.

Tubby became zealous in his pursuit of Toc H and was always
moving forward to endeavor to endeavor and would repeat, "After
that, we begin to begin, which is all man ever does." Tubby's unique
approach to his fellowman never changed, it remained simple: to trust
them, and this became the single most important ingredient decisive to
the success of the Toc H Movement. It gave the Movement kinetic
energy and empowered individuals and groups to move forward, to act
and to venture out. He started by recruiting those men who had
registered their names on a posted list at the entry to the Upper Room,
meaning everyone on this golden list, at one time or another made it to
the sanctuary. Those lists filled two large sand bags and included the
names and addresses of thousands of men. When the house was
ordered to close and evacuated during the Third Battle of Ypres, one
of the bags disappeared, never to be found again. The one remaining
sand bag contained some 4,000 slips of paper. Names entered without
any designation of rank such as Colonel, Captain, Corporal or Private,
emanating from the infamous sign posted over Tubby's office
doorway: "All rank abandon, ye who enter here." Tubby knew the
value of this mailbag. He personally carried it back to England and in
the upcoming years it rarely left his side.

Many of the men in the sandbag had been killed, others were
scattered throughout England and the world. Tubby kept to his
impossible schedule of averaging only three hours of sleep a night and
after retiring from a full day of activities, the post-midnight hours were
reserved for writing till the wee hours of dawn. When he retired to his
room, he'd open his "sandbag" and commence his evening exercise of
personally penning letter after letter, bringing his heart and mind to

hand, and hand to pen, and pen to paper. These were deeply personal letters and how could anyone, having experienced the horror of the trenches and the hope and joy of Talbot House refuse? Many didn't. Often Tubby penned more than forty letters each night. A call from the Good Padre to commit thyself to service, based on the renewing of oneself as in Romans 12:2 - "Do not conform any longer to the pattern of this world but be transformed by the renewing of your mind." To his delight, should a letter be answered, he'd respond with another.

The actual groundwork for the development of Toc H was through arduous, personalized letter writing, speaking engagements and newspaper articles, while Tubby devoted himself in keeping the names and addresses of anyone who showed the slightest bit of interest. The list of supporters grew and soon, throughout the United Kingdom, the inauspicious name of Toc H was cropping up in pubs, churches, on the street and within family circles.

Tubby remained completely unaccustomed to the meaning of the word "No." Besides, Tubby knew something: he had experienced the bare bones nature of men and knew what brought them to their knees. He had learned, oh so well, how to communicate with them. He knew their fears, their hopes and their aspirations. He knew within those experiences there was faith, and from that he believed he could tap into men's convictions.

It was not without struggle that Tubby pursued his impudent dream of Toc H. And with all things new came an infinitum of problems and challenges. In 1919 he wrote, "Like many other men possessed by dreams, I took my plans, my projects, my absurdities to many men; most of them turned me down. I became bitter, chilled and disappointed." From within that constant state of struggle Tubby became even more determined. When Tubby feared failure for the lack of necessary funds, he approached his cousin and friend, Dick Sheppard, the vicar of St. Martin-in-the-Field at Trafalgar Square in London. When they met, Dick took Tubby by the hand, sat him down and said, "Tubby, before we start to talk, I want to tell you that I have prayed for you and for Talbot House day after day since I first heard of it. Come let us pray together." And they did. "Therefore, I tell you, whatever you ask for in prayer, believe that you have received it, and it will be yours." - Mark 11:24

Reverend Sheppard knew what Tubby wanted, a house in London and a good sum of money to start with. "Of course," Dick added, "I can't say how it will come in, but I am quite sure it will. The work is God's... please remember, Tubby, that everything does happen which God means; and I am quite sure He means Talbot House. When would you like to come and talk to my people?" Tubby spoke passionately of his dreams and of the needs to the body at St. Martins. His prayers were answered as the first L10,000 came from two worshipers. From those kind and generous donations, the first Talbot House for Toc H opened at Red Lion Square in London in 1919. Tubby was back in the inn keeping business, minus the World at War. He named it "Mark I" and this first house was modeled after Talbot House with beds for guests and Tubby saying, "An inn without beds is like a song without a chorus."

Tubby wanted all the world to know Talbot House had been transplanted in London, whether it be by word of mouth, his after-midnight letter writing campaign, telegrams, speaking engagements in Anglican churches, newspaper articles and even from the people on the street who would attest to the uproarious laughter and song originating from the new Talbot House.

Although Toc H now had a house to start with, Tubby made it clear men's souls were not won through architecture. From his experiences on the field of battle, Tubby knew worship could take place anywhere, at any time and under any circumstances. From the beginning of the Toc H Movement, Tubby encouraged the Gospel to go forward in earnest conversation, not only at Mark I but everywhere: in offices, the streets, the workshops, the docks, the mills, the shops, the pubs and most importantly, Tubby encouraged it to go forward in the homes.

Once opened, the first Mark never lacked for guests. What it did lack for was money. These were difficult times with unemployment and soup lines being the sign of the times. Soldiers, who had fought when their country called them, returned home to find themselves a burden on society and stood in endless unemployment lines. Tubby saw a new and different battlefield emerge; a battlefield of temptation, alcohol, loneliness, unemployment, homelessness and despair. The first task was to find jobs for those who risked their lives for their country. Toc H started by assessing the abilities of its members, the needs of the community and endeavored to match the two together.

They became so successful they were called "The Job Master" and became an employment center. Within a year, more houses opened in London, Manchester and Southampton (Mark 2, 3 & 4). When people were not within easy traveling distance to a Mark, a network of local groups would meet in homes, churches and public halls.

There was confusion regarding the direction, objectives and goals of Toc H, but from its origin, it was clear, the aim was to bring people together, and in doing so, to bring the spirit of Christ to life within the individual through personal contact and social service. Toc H did not start with a Mission Statement, a Board of Directors, Bylaws or the typical trappings of what organizations do to stay or become organized. Toc H was to be different from its very onset to its inner workings. However, even as a Movement, Toc H needed some direction to guide it.

The earliest statement for the direction of Toc H was drawn up by Tubby Clayton, Reverend Dick Sheppard and Alexander Patterson in 1920. The Movement would be guided by the Four Points of the Toc H Compass:

1. FRIENDSHIP: To love widely. To provide members with opportunities to develop a spirit of understanding and reconciliation. Members are called on: To welcome all in friendship. To lessen by habit of thought, word and deed the prejudices which divide people. To see the needs of others as their own.

2. SERVICE: To build bravely. To enable members, with their varying gifts, to serve their fellows. Members are called on: To give personal service. To study local and international conditions and their effect on others, and by their example to challenge their neighbors to seek the way of Christ.

3. FAIR MINDEDNESS: To think fairly. To bring to members the knowledge and experience of others. Members are called on: To listen always to the views of others and to find their own convictions. To influence public opinion so that conflict may be lessened by sympathetic and intelligent understanding.

> 4. THE KINGDOM OF GOD: To witness humbly. To work for a better world through the example of friendship, service and fair mindedness. Members are called on: To acknowledge the spiritual nature of man, to help the truth prevail and to practice the Christian way of life.

And just what was this Toc H? Alexander Patterson wrote, "A gathering of young men who seek to rebuild a broken world with the mortar of comradeship and the bricks, the solid bricks, of personal service. There is no true comradeship without surrender, no true service without sacrifice. We hope to carry on a holy and ceaseless war against pride and snobbery wherever we meet them. In the spirit of Jesus Christ we are joined together, and we shall go forward setting our course not on the waves but by the stars."

In December of 1922, a group of Toc H delegates gathered to affirm their faith. During that momentous gathering, Peter Monie drafted the Main Resolution of Toc H: "Remembering with gratitude how God used the Old House to bring home to multitudes of men that behind the ebb and flow of things temporal stand the eternal realities, and to send them forth strengthened to fight at all costs for the setting up of His Kingdom upon Earth: we pledge ourselves to strive to listen now and always for the voice of God; to know His Will revealed in Christ and to do it fearlessly, reckoning nothing of the world's opinion or its successes for ourselves or this our family; and toward this end, to think fairly, to love widely, to witness humbly and to build bravely."

All too often, Tubby had witnessed firsthand the death and destruction of the youth and future of England. He had been surrounded by death and it was the loss of young lives that impacted Tubby the most. The ones who would never have the opportunity to marry, experience the joys of life, to be a husband, a father, a grandfather. The loss of youth through death is not only the tragic loss of life, it is the loss of a life not yet lived.

Toc H insisted attitudes of authority, superiority and distinction of rank or class be abandoned before entering the fellowship of its society. Men must meet each other on common ground if humanity is to build a social order capable of overcoming the strains of the future.

In his wisdom, Tubby realized if Toc H were to become a "reminiscent group" of the war, it was doomed to failure. For growth and vitality to occur they needed to widely embrace, include and appeal to the youth of the day. It would have to touch their hearts and minds in a way that would stimulate them, offer them hope, influence their character, instill confidence and move them to action. Tubby reasoned, "I would beseech that we should not be unduly pessimistic about the younger people coming on. We cannot wrap them up in cotton wool; we cannot hope to curb them with any negative code; but once we can enlist them in a cause which gives them each a real responsibility, we have done more to straighten out their lives than could be done by any multitude of cautionary tales." Soon, Toc H was running Boys Clubs and operating youth centers.

The mind needs to be stimulated and Tubby encouraged discussions on religion, science, politics, art, commerce and worldly affairs, with humor and laughter always being one of the main ingredients. Discussions were promoted and questions were asked, "Just what actions should be taken to help a situation or a given circumstance?" The Toc H approach was to take a practical and realistic approach; just what was needed in each community, then set out to do it, right then and there.

Speaking of speaking, Tubby had learned something about the art of addressing groups, saying each speaker should address a single theme, taking about ten minutes to express it. The speaker should be careful not to vary too much as the truth was usually pretty basic to understand. Tubby could dress a truth in many garments, but he was careful not to make it too complex or obscure, therefore, no matter how often the subject was discussed or the story was told, the main content always remained the same. Tubby's magic tip to all public speakers who addressed audiences with the same topic was to "Never pick-up the parcel (the topic or story) by the same piece of string which you carried it the previous day or week! Start anywhere you like, go forwards, backwards, start in the middle, start before the beginning–anywhere–but never start at the same place." This advice gave the rest needed from repeating the same story over and over again. It kept the speaker on his or her toes, keeping them conscious to think carefully about what was told and how to keep telling the same story from a fresh perspective. Tubby's best advice: "Do not aspire to amplify your statement. Let it grow more direct as it proceeds; begin at a fresh point on each occasion; vary the length of time which you devote to this or that facet of the solid center; and always, 'Sit down before they wish you to sit down!'"

With the focus on youth and the promotion of discussion groups crossing the barriers of age, gender and social class, Tubby offered valuable advice, "One of the chief difficulties with arguing with the young, is that the young will argue back!" Yet, healthy discussion was a vital process leading to healthy debate and often compromise, reconciliation and resolution. The basis of lively discussion within the Movement was always to unite and understand, not to separate. Tubby's vision was to be inspired by making new friends. "Launch out," he proclaimed. "Find more friends and listen to what they say."

Tubby remained undeterred in promoting Toc H. He was exhausted at times, even to the point of becoming seriously ill. Yet again, he was driven and exhilarated by the continuous discovery of himself and the renewal of his faith through the discovery of others. He propelled this diverse movement forward, like a modern-day version of John the Baptist on a mad dash to spread the word—like the Gospel, the Good News—about Toc H. He went from London to Edinburgh, Newcastle, Manchester, Leeds, Birmingham, Liverpool, Sheffield, Portsmouth, Brighton, Northampton, Bristol, Oxford and Cambridge, whether by train, taxi, coach, foot, bicycle or horseback. Soon volunteers from all walks of life were joining and with them came the expertise needed.

After World War I, Talbot House reverted back to its owner, Coevoet Camerlynck, while what took place there spread throughout the world. Tubby became good friends with Lord Charles Wakefield, the British philanthropist and businessman who patented Castrol Oil, the household name for oil used in automobiles, airplanes and motorcycles. In 1929, through the generosity of Lord Wakefield, Talbot House was purchased, and an Anglo-Belgium Talbot House Association was formed to care for its continued operation as a living, historic testimony to what it represented. Many of the old furnishings, notices and artifacts of the house were returned, along with updating the plumbing.

Within the first ten years more than 400 branches were started throughout Britain and more than 200 branches overseas. Wherever Tubby was, he was accompanied by his Greek New Testament and he never missed midday prayers. His infectious and exhilarating vision spread, and the membership grew beyond his wildest dreams. Many prominent people supported the Movement and by 1938 there were more than 1,000 branches in Britain and another 400 branches worldwide. He was back in his unique method of inn keeping and a golden age of hostelry flourished throughout England—throughout the world. One of the grand results of the Toc H Movement was anyone arriving in any part of the English-speaking world who notified Toc H of their presence would be met by new friends, housed, entertained, fed and shown the ropes of the area through an atmosphere of friendship. No matter how far away their job or life would take them, whether to the Australian bush or jungles of Africa, Toc H would stay in touch. For all who traveled and volunteered, wherever Toc H was, there was a home!

Tubby visited members in South Africa and toured thirty leper colonies. He was moved by what he saw and wrote, "Here there were human beings without hope, some without limbs and many of them blind. I who had never hitherto beheld a leper in my life, now saw a nightmare laid out before me under the unrelenting menace of the sun. Some of them gasped and cried aloud for water. Others were like the witches in Macbeth stirring their evening meal; women among them clutched enfeebled children close to their breasts. From that time onward leprosy became a nightmare in my mind without redress." Upon Tubby's return to London he made an impassioned plea for volunteers to train and devote five years of their life to work with lepers in Africa. Within six months fifty people volunteered. Toc H joined forces with the British Empire Leprosy Relief Association (BELRA) and sent volunteers to Africa and India. Today BELRA is known as LEPRA Health in Action and has been one of the world's leading health organizations associated with leprosy along with the treatment of tuberculosis, HIV and malaria. Regarding this work, one of the original Toc H volunteers in 1930 wrote, "Toc H has taken up one of the finest pieces of work since the abolition of slavery."

From the start, Tubby and Toc H caught the attention of the Royal Family who became official sponsors. Prince Albert George, affectionately known as "Bertie" to his family was the second son of King George V. On numerous unsuccessful occasions he attempted to court the Duchess of York, Elizabeth Angela Marguerite Bowes-Lyon.

Bertie fell in love with Elizabeth and proposed to her twice but she would have nothing to do with it as she enjoyed her freedom. On one occasion, after she rebuffed Albert's proposal, she said if she were to marry into the Royal Family, she was "afraid never again to be free to think, speak and act as I feel I really ought to." However, Prince Albert was in love and proclaimed, "I will marry no other." When Albert's mother, Queen Mary realized the depth of her son's love for this "legal commoner," she decided to see for herself who this girl was who had stolen her son's heart. After numerous visits with Elizabeth, she too became convinced this was the one girl who could make her Bertie happy.

Elizabeth was born into a family of Scottish nobility. Her father inherited the Earldom of Strathmore and Kinghorne in 1904. Growing up she spent much of her childhood at Glamis Castle, the Earl's ancestral home. When she was eight, she was sent off to attend private school in London. On her fourteenth birthday, when Britain declared war on Germany, she returned home to Glamis Castle. Here, at a young and impressionable age, her home was turned into a military hospital for wounded soldiers including those from the Western Front. Along with her mother and elder sister Rosie, Elizabeth worked and helped manage the hospital. She cared for the soldiers, enjoyed personal contact with them, helped them write letters to loved ones and played cards with the men. Elizabeth learned to relate to people of all backgrounds and social classes as the wounds of war have no barriers or class distinctions. Then came the loss of her beloved older brother, Fergus, an officer killed in action at the Battle of Loos in 1915.

Elizabeth tried to keep a respectable distance from Albert, remembering her father's admonition, "To avoid royal entanglements at all costs." However, Prince Albert was persistent and would not take "No" for an answer. Elizabeth saw within him the character of a man she loved. On January 13, 1923, as they walked together in the woods at St. Paul's Walden Bury, Albert proposed for a third time, and on this occasion, Elizabeth agreed to become his wife. Three months later, the couple married at Westminster Abbey. The marriage was controversial because only English royalty had married into the English Royal Family during the past one hundred plus years. Princes were expected to marry Princesses and Elizabeth was no Princess. Even as the Duchess of York, she was considered a "legal commoner."

On the day of their wedding, Elizabeth won everyone over when she stopped and laid her wedding bouquet on the Tomb of the Unknown Warrior, the tomb which holds an unidentified British soldier killed on the battlefield during World War I. It was a subtle and beautiful gesture on the day she was entering a new life, remembering those who had fought and lost their lives for their country. Since then, this gesture has become a tradition, where every royal bride, upon entering or departing Westminster Abbey has laid their wedding bouquet at the Tomb of the Unknown Warrior.

In 1926 the couple had their first child, a daughter, Elizabeth II. On January 20, 1936, Albert's father, King George V died, and succession of the throne passed to Albert's older brother, the Prince of Wales. The coronation of the new King was scandalous as Edward was having an intimate affair with Mrs. Wallace Simpson, an American who was on her second marriage. Simpson obtained her second divorce, however, the Church of England would not recognize it. For the King to marry such a person was not only scandalous, it was against the laws of the Church of which the King was the figurehead. However, King Edward VIII declared he was going to marry, "The woman I love." The Archbishop of Canterbury strongly opposed the union and advised Edward the people of England would never accept an American divorcee as their Queen. After Simpson was granted her second divorce, King Edward became the first British monarch to voluntarily abdicate the throne and married Wallace. Albert reluctantly was forced to become King by default and advised to use the royal name of George VI in succession to his father. The Royal Coronation Ceremony was held on May 12, 1937, where he and Elizabeth were crowned the King and Queen of Great Britain, Ireland and the British dominions, beyond the seas and Emperor and Empress of India. Edward's marriage to Simpson continued to be scandalous, especially in 1937 when they visited Germany and were personal guests of Adolf Hitler.

During the Blitz, the Luftwaffe—Germany's modern and powerful air force—conducted indiscriminate aerial bombing of London. One night, the Luftwaffe dropped 10,000 incendiary bombs in their attempt to burn London to the ground. For their safety, the King and Queen were advised to leave London and send their children to Canada. But the Queen publicly stated, "The children won't go without me. I won't leave the King. And the King will never leave." Elizabeth would often walk the streets of bombed and burnt out areas, especially the East End where the oldest Church in London, All Hallows stood. When her home at Buckingham Palace took direct hits during the height of the bombing, Elizabeth said, "I'm glad we've been bombed. It makes me feel I can look the East End in the face." Queen Elizabeth had such a strong impact on British morale, Adolf Hitler noted she was "the most dangerous woman in Europe."

Reverend Tubby Clayton was appointed Chaplain to King George V, King George VI, and Queen Elizabeth II. He developed a close and abiding friendship with King George VI and his wife, Queen Elizabeth. On February 6, 1952, King George VI died of lung cancer, making way for their eldest daughter, Elizabeth II to become Queen and for Elizabeth to become the "Queen Mother" or later as she was revered, "The Queen Mum." During her tenure as Queen and Queen Mum she was loved by most all of Great Britain. She was Patron to the Toc H Women's Association and a great friend and supporter throughout Tubby's life. Elizabeth was 101 when she died on July 24, 2003, and had lived longer than any member of the Royal Family in British history. On the day of her funeral, more than a million people filled the streets outside Westminster Abbey and along the twenty-three-mile route her funeral procession took to her final resting place, beside her husband at St. George's Chapel at Windsor Castle. At her request, the funeral wreath laid on top of her coffin was placed at the Tomb of the Unknown Warrior in Westminster Abbey by her daughter, Queen Elizabeth II.

Tubby's knowledge of the world came from his wartime relationships with Canadians, Australians, Americans and New Zealanders. For Toc H to spread beyond the shores of England he needed to travel overseas. His first call was to Canada, where there was interest to join Toc H, and from Canada, it was off to the United States. The Movement then spread to Australia, New Zealand, South Africa, West Africa, Jerusalem, Tel-Aviv, Cairo, Alexandria, Benghazi, Tripoli, Tunis, Malaya and the Far East.

A Ceremony of Light was created where a few moments of silence were observed in memory of all the old friends who had sacrificed their lives and who had been left behind in the Salient or elsewhere from the ravages of war. To this ceremony a lamp was added, modeled after the oil lamp used by the first Christians hiding in the catacombs of Rome after the crucifixion of Christ. A lamp with a single flame representing God's light inscribed in Latin with Psalm 36:9, "In lumine Tuo videbimus lumen - In Thy light shall we see light." The lamp became the symbol of Toc H.

Tubby met Coleman Jennings, the same Coleman Jennings who was a personal aide to President Wilson at Versailles. The two realized they had many friends in common, including the Royal Family. Coleman and Tubby developed a close friendship. In 1924, Coleman became active in Toc H by starting the Washington, D.C. branch. Tubby would stay at Coleman's home in D.C. and Coleman would spend time with Tubby in England. Within themselves they discovered a deep connection and navigated their lives and resources towards helping others.

The armistice that stopped the fighting of World War I, followed by the Treaty of Versailles was only a temporary impasse. Back in Germany, Adolf Hitler blamed the Jews for much of Germany's defeat. He believed Jews controlled the German press and in doing so were able to control public opinion. When World War I turned towards Germany's ultimate defeat, the press reported the news depicting how difficult life in the devastated Fatherland had become. Hitler viewed this as a traitorous, Jewish act, demoralizing his country and their fighting forces, when in reality, the press was only reporting the truth and futility of the war. In Hitler's book *Mein Kampf (My Struggle)* he wrote, "Now the time had come to take steps against the whole treacherous brotherhood of the Jewish poisoners of the people. Now was the time to deal with them summarily without the slightest consideration for any screams and complaints that might arise... If the best men were dying at the front, the least we could do was to wipe out the vermin. ...The mightiest counterpart to the Aryan is represented by the Jew." Hitler hated the Jews and his description of them said, "He is and remains the typical parasite, a sponger who like a noxious bacillus keeps spreading as soon as a favorable medium invites him. And the effect of his existence is also like that of spongers: whenever he appears, the host people dies out after a shorter or longer period." Hitler became the most evil man the world has ever experienced, a devil of a man who said, "I am convinced that I am acting as the agent of our Creator. By fighting off the Jews, I am doing the Lord's work."

In the year leading up to D-Day, there were 300 Toc H service clubs in the United Kingdom with 30,000 volunteers and 120 Toc H clubs overseas. Although much of their manpower had been depleted by the call to arms, Toc H played a vital and crucial role providing needed services throughout the bombings and devastations of World War II. During a one-month period in 1943, Toc H provided needed social services for some 3,729,687 including lodging and beds for 20,000.

Toc H groups started in German and Japanese POW camps in Burma, China, Nigeria and Malaysia. Frank Miles, an office clerk with the British Army was captured in Singapore when the city fell to the Japanese. From there he was taken to Changi, an island where the conditions in the POW camp were deplorable and the diet limited to small portions of rice and water. Disease and malnutrition was rampant amongst the prisoners, they were hungry and weak all the time. Small concrete cells built for one person with a single concrete slab for a bed were crammed with four prisoners to a cell. Frank recalled, "You were touching the walls and each other all the time. And the bugs! They came at you at night and there was nothing you could do about it. With the heat and the overcrowding everyone suffered from dysentery and malaria—which became so common it was regarded as a common cold." It was a work camp and prisoners were sent away to build railways. Many never returned. A Toc H group was formed, and members visited and helped care for the sick and dying. To keep morale up, each week they held a meeting which included a guest speaker, usually a fellow Toc H'er who'd speak within their area of expertise, something completely unrelated to their wartime misery, such as the future of plastics, the future of health care, or a touching story of a family Christmas in Wales, something, anything to keep their minds active and off the misery at hand. Soldiers of all ranks mixed, and communal prayers were shared. Minutes to the meetings were taken and a Toc H Lamp was made.

The POW camp had a hospital. Chaplain F.H. Stallard received permission from the Japanese commander to convert part of the ground floor of the hospital's dysentery wing to a chapel dedicated to Saint Luke the Physician. Stanley Warren, a British bombardier, while sick with dysentery used charcoal from fire pits, chalk, camouflage paint and other creative materials to paint five murals in the chapel: the Nativity, the Ascension, the Crucifixion, the Last Supper and St. Luke in Prison. The murals lifted the spirits of the POWs, the sick and dying. Stanley would not sign any of them and considered them "a gift to God."

The British army fought their way to Burma in February 1942 and Singapore fell. The prisoners looked forward to their emancipation and plans were made to safely guard their Toc H Minutes and the Toc H Lamp. They were taken back to England and have been preserved for more than seventy-five years. In 1988 a television documentary was made inviting prisoners of the Changi POW camp to return to Singapore. Frank was unable to make the trip. Former POW, Wally Hammond made the trip along with Stanley Warren. Wally presented the Toc H Lamp they made while held captive and when presented said, "When lit it symbolizes the spirit of light which its members should show amongst all people, that they may see good work being done, and glorify 'Our Father who is in Heaven.'"

During the German Blitz the historic church at All Hallows took many direct hits and was all but destroyed, leaving only the shell of the tower, some bare stone walls and the crypt intact. After the war, the restorative branch of the government concluded the oldest church in London had sustained too much damage to be restored. All Hallows had tremendous history and for Tubby it had family history. After the war and the destruction of All Hallows, the restoration and reconstruction of the old church became Tubby's next great passion.

All Hallows had a bloody past due to its proximity to the Tower of London where the church received the bodies of beheaded prisoners for burial. Back in the 1500s, King Henry VIII opposed paying taxes and fees to the Catholic Church in Rome, plus he wanted a son and would marry eight wives, insisting on annulments and divorces whenever things didn't work out. The Catholic Church would not cooperate with his repeated requests and King Henry decided to separate from Rome, creating the Anglican Church of England which he would head. Sir Thomas Moore, the Catholic humanist, author and Lord Chancellor refused to acknowledge Henry as head of the church and his second marriage to Anne Boleyn. Henry and Thomas had been great friends, yet Henry had Thomas arrested, tried and found guilty of high treason against the King. Thomas was imprisoned in the Tower, beheaded and buried at All Hallows in 1555.

Not only was All Hallows the oldest church in London, it had historic ties to the United States. William Penn was baptized at All Hallows in 1644. His father, Sir Admiral William Penn served in the Royal Navy and fought during the English Civil War. During the Great Fire of London in 1666, eighty-seven churches including St. Paul's Cathedral and most of the government houses along with the homes of 70,000 in a city of 80,000, were burned to the ground. During the fire, All Hallows was saved by Admiral Penn who had the buildings surrounding All Hallows demolished to create a firebreak. His son became a close friend to George Fox, founder of the Quakers. Fox refused to take up arms on religious grounds, nor would he swear allegiance to Oliver Cromwell or to the King because of his interpretation of the Gospel of Matthew: "But I tell you, Do not swear at all: either by heaven, for it is God's throne; or by earth, for it is His footstool; or by Jerusalem, for it is the city of the Great King."

William Penn was expelled from the Church of England and arrested for preaching in a public square to a gathering of fellow Quakers. The Lord Mayor of London presided as judge at Penn's trial and directed the jury to deliver a verdict of "Guilty." However, when the jury delivered their verdict of "Not Guilty," the incensed Lord Mayor responded, "If that be your verdict, your verdict be damned" and had Penn and the entire jury locked up. From jail, Penn and the jury fought back and were successful in securing the right for all English juries to be free from the control of judges and not be judged just on the facts of the case, but to be judged based on the law itself. Most importantly, Penn established the right for men and women to be considered "innocent until proven guilty." That case became famous and helped shape the foundation of the American legal and justice system and is credited with creating habeas corpus, the legal means of freeing those unlawfully held in prison.

The persecution of the Quakers for their beliefs was fierce. William decided to establish a new and free Quaker settlement in the British Colonies on land transferred to him by King Charles II, resulting from a large debt the King owed to William's deceased father that help fund the English Civil War. William wanted to call his colony "Sylvania" which is Latin for "woods" but the King insisted on naming it Pennsylvania in honor of Admiral Penn. William founded the colony of Quaker pilgrims in Pennsylvania on March 4, 1681 with a Charter of Liberties guarantying fair trials and religious freedom. In doing so, he became one of the founding fathers of the United States, an early champion of religious freedom and democracy, and his democratic principles served as the inspiration for the U.S. Constitution.

The first President of the United States was George Washington. The second President was John Adams. His son, John Quincy Adams, during a diplomatic trip to London in 1795 fell in love with Louisa Catherine Johnson. They were married at All Hallows in 1797 and John Quincy Adams became the sixth President of the United States in 1825. After his term ended in 1829, John Quincy Adams did something no American President has ever done and was elected to Congress, serving in the House of Representatives for the state of Massachusetts until his death in 1848. During his time in Congress he was asked to defend forty-three black men and woman who had been imprisoned after they were discovered on August 26, 1839 off the eastern tip of Long Island on a flagless, tattered ship by the name of Amistad. A long and historic legal case commenced regarding the status of these blacks. "Were these Amistads slaves or free men and women?" The case made its way to the U.S. Supreme Court, where five of the sitting nine Justices were Southern slave owners.

John Quincy Adams searched his heart regarding his ability to do justice to their cause and when asked, he answered, "By the blessing of God I will argue the case before the Supreme Court." When John met the blacks, he shook their hands and said, "God willing, we will make you free." In October 1840 he wrote in his diary, "I implore the mercy of God to control my temper, to enlighten my soul and to give me utterance, that I may prove myself in every respect equal to the task." In his summary argument before the highest court in the land, he attacked the southern intellectual defense of slavery and he quoted the Declaration of Independence by saying, "The moment you come to the Declaration, that every man has a right to life and liberty, an inalienable right, this case is decided. I ask nothing more in behalf of these unfortunate men than this Declaration." Adams ended his Supreme Court summation on a brilliant challenging note, one that tested the moral fiber and character of each sitting justice by saying,

"In taking, then, my final leave of this Bar, and of this Honorable Court, I can only ejaculate a fervent petition to Heaven, that every member of it may go to his final account with as little of earthly frailty to answer for as those illustrious dead (in reference to the previous Justices who had died and gone to meet their maker), and that you may, every one, after the close of a long and virtuous career in this world, be received at the portals of the next with the approving sentence: 'Well done, good and faithful servant; enter thou into the joy of the Lord.'" John Quincy Adams appealed to the judges as God Fearing Christians, challenging them to face their own eternal judgment and reminding them that one day, they too would be judged. On March 9, 1841, the Supreme Court announced their landmark decision, the Amistads were indeed kidnapped Africans and entitled to their freedom.

Tubby had been unsuccessful at home in raising funds to restore All Hallows, yet he promised to have the Church rebuilt and established what was known as "squatter's rights" at the shell of All Hallows by bringing in a token supply of building materials. Always in search of money for the causes he promoted, Tubby found Coleman Jennings was in a position to help. The Jennings family walked in the circles of Presidents, Senators, Congressmen, Kings and Queens, Countesses, Ambassadors and Bishops. Coleman understood and appreciated what money could accomplish when it came to worthy causes and, he not only had access to family money—he knew how to fundraise. They had much in common, including their epic efforts dedicated to the construction of two historic churches; Tubby's rebuilding and restoration of All Hallows in London and Coleman's magnificent fifty-year role in the construction of the National Cathedral in Washington, D.C. Inspired by John Winant, the Ambassador of the United States to the Court of St. James (U.S. Ambassador to the U.K.), and with the help and connections from Jennings and many others, Tubby was successful in raising funds and supplies. From the U.S. he received financial donations and steel; from Canada - timber and floor tiles; from Australia - steam pipes; and from Rhodesia - copper for the spire. With Tubby leading the way, reconstruction of the oldest church in London began.

In 1948, the Queen Mother laid the new foundation stone signifying the rebuilding of the historic church. Years later, Tubby escorted the

Queen Mother into the Church where thirty Toc H Volunteers were present, the Lord Mayor of London and the Bishop of London. He led the Queen Mum to a chair constructed from the original pulpit door of 1613 and there, the Queen Mum sat in attendance as the rededication service began. Tubby went on to become the Vicar of All Hallows which became the Home (Guild) Church for Toc H. The vicarage at All Hallows became Tubby's primary residence.

In 1938, President Franklin Roosevelt appointed Joseph Kennedy to the Court of St. James as the U.S. Ambassador to the United Kingdom. When World War II started, Ambassador Kennedy argued against giving military and economic aid to the United Kingdom. He also had personal reasons for wanting to avoid war: three of his sons; Joe, John and Bobby were all eligible to serve. Joe Kennedy, Sr. had plenty of money and the ego to go with it, plus he had his own designs on becoming President of the United States. He tried to arrange meetings with Hitler to improve relations with the U.S. and opined, "Democracy is finished in England." He fled from London to the countryside during the nightly bombings and became extremely unpopular amongst the British. With pressure from the Roosevelt administration he resigned in November, 1940, his presidential aspirations in ruins.

Joe's eldest son, Joe Kennedy, Jr., enlisted, became a naval pilot, completed twenty-five combat missions then volunteered for a mission where his aircraft, heavily loaded with bombs was to be flown directly into a German missile site while Kennedy and his skeleton crew were to parachute moments before detonation. Two minutes before the planned bailout, the bombs exploded prematurely, vaporizing all aboard. Joe's second son, John, with the help of his father's money became the first Roman Catholic President of the United States and was assassinated in Dallas, Texas on November 22, 1963. Robert Kennedy, the third son, became a Senator for the state of New York and ran for President in 1968. His campaign quickly gained momentum and after winning California was on the threshold of securing the Democratic ticket. He gave his victory speech at the Ambassador Hotel in Los Angeles on June 5, 1968, and when exiting the hotel was shot three times and assassinated by Sirhan Sirhan who said he felt betrayed by Kennedy's support for Israel. The youngest son, Edward "Ted" Kennedy served forty-seven years in the U.S. Senate for Massachusetts.

After Joe Kennedy resigned, President Roosevelt appointed John Gilbert Winant as the Ambassador of the United States to the Court of St. James. Winant's heart was with the common man and he was a friend of Coleman Jennings. He was a deep thinker, a Republican, an idealist, a brooder and a dreamer prone to bouts of depression. He stood tall, lean and strong, a quiet, shy man, yet he could be extremely engaging. With thick black hair and eyebrows, penetrating dark eyes, an angular face, he resembled Abraham Lincoln. In 1917, during World War I, he enlisted with the American Expeditionary Forces, became a pilot and Commander of the 8th Observation Squadron in France. When he returned home he entered politics. He served New Hampshire in the House of Representatives and as a Senator. At the age of thirty-six, Winant became the youngest Governor in the state's history and served three terms, two during the Great Depression. He was one of the few governors to reach across party lines. He walked from his home to the Governor's office, greeting people on his way and handing out money to the poor until his pockets were empty. President Roosevelt appointed Winant chair of the Social Security Board, asked him to negotiate labor disputes and appointed him Assistant Director of the International Labor Organization at the League of Nations in Geneva in 1935.

Just prior to leaving for Great Britain Winant gave a speech saying, "...The pillars of our republic, the sinews of democracy, have to do with the right of free speech, the right peaceably to assemble, the right of a free press, habeas corpus, trial by jury and the right to worship according to our conscience. In the aggressor countries, and in every country dominated by the aggressor countries, all these rights have been wiped out. There is no right of free speech, no right peaceably to assemble, no right of free press and a denial of freedom to worship. All men are subject to arrest at will without trial by twelve good men and true. All those things that men have fought for here in this country, all those things that have made America what it is, are being destroyed in Europe. We are today the arsenal of democracy, the service of supply against the aggressor nations. Great Britain has asked that we give them tools that they may finish the job. We can stand with them as free men in the comradeship of hard work, not asking but giving, with unity of purpose in defense of liberty under law, of government answerable to the people. In a just cause, and with God's goodwill, we can do no less."

It was after The Battle of Britain when Winant arrived in London exclaiming, "I'm very glad to be here. There is no place I'd rather be at this time than in England." It was just what the Brits needed to hear from the American Ambassador. The story of Winant's arrival was carried on the front pages of almost every newspaper throughout Great Britain and contrary to his predecessor, who fled to the safety of the countryside, Winant stayed in London during the nighttime raids. He walked the streets and saw the devastation rained down from Germany's incessant aerial bombings of civilian populations. He walked the streets with Winston Churchill, and he walked the streets with Tubby Clayton and witnessed the bombed-out destruction of All Hallows and the surrounding East End which was hanging on in desperate poverty. John Winant and Tubby became friends. They spoke of the future and of a program where young Americans would come to London as volunteers to work in the East End. Winant told Tubby he'd accompany him to American colleges to recruit volunteers and help raise funds to rebuild All Hallows.

In 1940, fighting again returned to Belgium with the rapid advance of German troops. This time there was no line drawn and held along the Western Front. Five members of the Toc H staff at Talbot House were captured and taken prisoner. During the war, rumors spread that the sacred house had been destroyed. When Allied forces attacked the shores of France and drove the Germans back, the first Toc H member to re-enter Talbot House was BBC war correspondent, Frank Gillard who learned how the people of Poperinge, once again, preserved the contents of the house at great risk during the German occupation. The night before the Germans took possession of the house, four men came with horse and cart, removing everything in the house. Small objects were hidden in attics and cupboards and the Toc H Lamp was buried in the garden with only two people knowing its whereabouts. Larger objects were hidden in a cellar behind a false wall constructed to conceal them. The day the Germans retreated, it was feared the house had been booby-trapped. A local, Marcel de Rynck-Battheu courageously entered the house. The Germans had set the house on fire and Marcel found a bomb in the cellar. Marcel rallied the fire brigade, they put the fire out, removed the bomb and the house contents were returned as if they never left. In December 1944, Talbot House was reopened to the Allied troops in the area. Ten Poperinge women came regularly to help and make tea, and once again it was complete with soldiers of different rank and nationalities.

John Winant developed close relationships with King George VI, Queen Elizabeth and Prime Minister Churchill. He was at Chequers with Churchill on Dec. 7, 1941 when the chilling news of the bombing of Pearl Harbor arrived. Later Churchill said, "Mr. Winant always put the American point of view with force and clarity and argued his country's case with vigor, but his constant purpose was to smooth away the difficulties and prevent misunderstandings and he always gave us the feeling of how gladly he would give his life to see the good cause triumph... He was a friend of justice, truth and freedom."

President Truman awarded John Winant the "Presidential Medal of Merit" and King George VI bestowed Britain's highest civilian honor on him, "The Order of Merit." Honorary membership to this exclusive order has been awarded to only nine other individuals including General Dwight Eisenhower, Albert Schweitzer and Mother Teresa. When given, Queen Elizabeth told John, "You deserve it more than anyone." Winant also received honorable degrees from Oxford, Princeton, Dartmouth and Vassar.

Winant resigned his post as Ambassador to Great Britain in March 1946 and returned home. His wife, socialite Constance Russell became estranged over the years and while in England, John had an affair with Churchill's youngest daughter, Sarah. He told Sarah he wanted to divorce Constance and marry her. Sarah declined. Winant's life back home was filled with debt and disappointment and he became deeply depressed. On November 3, 1947, the day his book, Letter from Grosvenor Square was published, John Winant committed suicide at his home in Concord, New Hampshire.

Tubby would not let the tragic death of his friend stop what they had dreamed of, a program of youthful volunteers from the United States to Great Britain. In honor of his friend, Tubby named it "The Winant Volunteer Program" and keeping with the Tubby Clayton tradition, it was to be an adventure. The program was supported and promoted by Coleman Jennings with great enthusiasm and in the summer of 1948, with General Dwight Eisenhower as Chairman of the

Sponsoring Body, the first group of twenty-seven American and Canadian Winants crossed the Atlantic by ship and arrived in London. They arrived with confidence and laughter, full of enthusiasm and fun and took up shop in the East End. They taught crafts and new games, they worked at five Boys' Clubs, two local parishes including the bombed out remains of All Hallows and they paid for their own expenses. They were resourceful and devoted to whatever tasks given to them. Their energetic smiles were an infectious needed breath of fresh air sweeping through the streets, and the adrenalin of the Winant Volunteers helped the existing local youth leaders, and social workers, to "buck up" and get excited about their own jobs.

The average East Ender—the Cockney—are a proud and sensitive lot, quick to resent any acts of kindness that could be viewed as condescending patronage. But the Americans and Canadians didn't come across that way and remained indifferent to any local class distinctions. They were just too busy and excited about what they were doing to let anything stand in their way. Americans cut directly to the chase and as a consequence, were uniquely qualified to approach the Cockney with their inherent pride, ego and prejudices. The Canadians were laid back and let nothing interfere with their objectives. Together they jumped in, rolled up their sleeves, said "let's go" and went to work. The East Londoners couldn't help but take notice and soon they were living, working, playing and tipping a pint or two at the local pub with the Winant Volunteers.

Below Tower Hill was a popular beach where children swam and played on the River Thames. It had been patrolled by lifeguards, however by the end of August 1947, with the shortage of manpower, none were available. With the absence of lifeguards patrolling the river, during one weekend, five children drowned at the popular beach. When the first Winants arrived, they learned of the drownings, took the problem on and assured Tubby no more children would drown. They were as good as their word and from that point on, sent over an ongoing contingency of volunteer lifeguards to patrol the beach.

The Winant Volunteer Program thrived and during their summer visit to England, along with their work details, they were treated to an expansive view of life in Britain, including visits to Buckingham Palace and Royal Garden Parties with personal introductions to Tubby, the King and Queen. They visited Oxford University, the Tower of

London, the Houses of Parliament, Marlborough House, Canterbury Cathedral, Winston Churchill's home at Chartwell and the Toc H headquarters at Trinity Square where they exchanged stories, hopes and plans for the future with Toc H volunteers. By the time they returned home to the states, they had an incredible—and in many cases—life changing experience. In 1959, the program expanded and became a mutual exchange program where the Brits mirrored the Americans by sending British students to the States and Canada to perform volunteer social services. Tubby's name was added, and the international exchange program became known as the "Winant–Clayton Volunteer Program."

On D-Day, June 6, 1944, Alice Welford was staying in an English Toc H Service Club for women. After the war ended, Alice volunteered to go to Germany and work with Toc H staff. She was particularly affected by the plight of the German youth. Many of the schools had been destroyed, books were scarce, teachers were distraught, classes were huge and there was the lingering effects of their prior education from the Hitler Youth Movement, where they were commanded what to think. They had been treated as human products and forced into a regimented life. Their character had been robbed before it had the chance to develop. They were a blinded and disoriented generation of young people who had no idea of what it meant to have an open and honest relationship with each other. Alice saw them as a critical challenge; young people who wanted to learn how to identify with their feelings and how to openly discuss topics and issues with each other. Alice engaged them by promoting honest communications which spawned real relationships and she witnessed them revel in their own spirit of reconciliation.

It wasn't just the services organized and delivered by Toc H that excited people. It was the experience. Many had never seen people in real need before and were unaware of what it meant to be disadvantaged, disabled or poor. Through the process of getting involved, eyes were opened, opinions were changed, discussions were stimulated, and hearts were moved. Things happened; people could and did change for the better. Through service, Toc H challenged people to think about who they were, where they were headed and the meaning of their lives. In doing so, many learned to take risks, enjoy the journey of helping others and to accept, even rejoice in the diversity of those with whom they came in contact.

Toc H wanted to bring people together and defuse volatile situations through the understanding of others who appeared different; to find the common ground and reconcile. For real reconciliation to occur, there had to be respect on both sides and a willingness to be open and understand the other's point of view. The gathering of people from different walks of life; different social, economic, racial, religious and cultural backgrounds had to be more than an attempt to patronize the status quo, it needed to be an honest and genuine encounter between people who were opened to being challenged and changed. Toc H not only recognized this, they pursued it with tenacity. One of the instructions given by Jesus in the Gospel of Matthew is: "You shall love your neighbor as yourself." It is difficult enough to love our neighbors with the same amount of attention we devote to ourselves. But for Sue Coming it was different. She had no difficulty with the first part in loving her neighbor, it was the second part of loving herself where she admitted, "I find it terribly difficult to love me because I know me." Having been inspired by her first experience with a Toc H project to see life as an adventure, Sue graduated from college and went on to volunteer and teach in East Africa. Sue understood, "It was the spirit of volunteering at its best." During her time in Africa, Sue had an eye-opening experience and learned she could love herself by offering practical help to those in need.

Books and songs were written about Talbot House and the Toc H Movement. During the changing times of the 1960s Pink Floyd released their first album in August 1967, "The Piper at the Gates of Dawn." One of the songs: "Pow R Toc H." As Toc H progressed into the future, the pain and suffering from the war years were dissipating and with that, a new attitude towards social service was developing. Social needs and problems persisted as they always will. Within Toc H, the perspective and methodology of helping others was re-evaluated. No longer was it the notion of civic duty, social service or charity. The spirit of the Toc H experience was now compelling people to get "alongside" each other, including those in need. Instead of helping with the perspective of "We can help lift them up," it was changing to, "There is my brother, I must get alongside him and help."

In the 1960s and 1970s, Toc H developed the concept of "Projects," a variety of short-term work camps focused on young people achieving a constructive goal and operating as an adventure in the process. Along with these projects the post experiential discussion grew. Emphasis and structure was placed on the importance of these discussions, where everyone who worked together, afterwards, got together and discussed their experience. Stemming from the trenches of the Western Front, these post-op discussions—in true military fashion—were referred to as "debriefings." One of the advocates promoting this addition to the Toc H experience was the Birmingham Regional Director, John Mitchell.

John's wife, Jennifer volunteered for the Peace Corps and was a Clayton Volunteer in the states during the U.S. Civil Rights Movement. She marched on Washington, D.C. with the Reverend Dr. Martin Luther King, Jr. and later stated, "It was one of the most profound experiences of my life." Jennifer and John operated Mark #6 in Birmingham as a Toc H Project Center and residence for sixteen students and social workers. John Mitchell had an exceptional intellect, dual degrees and worked his way through the legal system becoming a solicitor-lawyer. He was motivated to address local social needs including the plight of gypsies whose civil rights were often violated. It was an unpopular position to take with surrounding communities hating Gypsies. With the help of Hilary Geater, a member of the Toc H staff, a school for itinerant Gypsy children was operated along with the Birmingham soup kitchen and a homeless shelter for men at St. Chad's Cathedral. John became the Regional Director and later, the National Director for Toc H. Hilary became an Editor for Toc H's "In Touch" magazine and a member of the Board of Directors.

Ken Butterfield, a social worker who worked with deaf people moved into Mark #6 and became involved with Toc H's Birmingham Outward Bound that took young people from all walks of life, including the deaf and those who had been in trouble with the law on adventure weekends, such as rock climbing and river rafting. Through those excursions of living, working and having an adventure together, social and class barriers were broken down and friendships formed. The Toc H Outward Bound program continues to this day.

For seventeen-year-old Liz Jones it happened during her second Toc H project. She worked with other teenagers including those who came from underprivileged backgrounds and together they helped decorate senior citizens homes. Her eyes were opened, and Liz said she nearly fell over when at the end of the week-long project, two leaders told her, "We think you could lead one of these things!" Liz thought to herself, "Me, look after two minibuses of teenagers, manage the project and everything else?" and thought, "They must be joking." It was the Tubby Clayton tradition of trusting and empowering others. A few months later, Liz attended a leader's training weekend and was informed which projects she would be leading.

Jane Richardson at twenty-three volunteered for the Winant-Clayton Exchange Program and as she put it, was "quite green" when she went to New York City to spend her summer working at Fountain House, a pioneering rehabilitation center for those suffering from mental illness. It was a work-in-progress with a skeleton staff overseeing 350 mentally ill residents who were held responsible for their daily operations including the cooking, the cleaning, even operating their own thrift shop and coffee bar. Jane came from a middle-class home in England. In New York City she lived in one of the worst neighborhoods where people were openly shooting heroin on the streets. Jane realized, "I was suddenly exposed to the whole American dream in all its monstrous manifestations. It was all heady stuff! And the residents (of Fountain House) showed me New York. They were caring for me. It was a relationship of equals." Jane spent four months there and thought the experience was "Wonderful; I was just bowled over." When she returned home, Jane was burning with enthusiasm and wanted to "spread the word" of this new community and interactive approach to mental health care. Jane knew she couldn't tolerate the entrenched bureaucratic approach by working for the British mental health care system. Instead, she joined the staff of Toc H and created support groups for the mentally ill and their families known as "Friendship Circles." Jane pursued her work with passion and perseverance. Her work grew and the "Friendship Circles" spread back to the United States with the first one opening in Cleveland in 1975.

Peter East had an infectious and humorous personality that could attract children from any culture. In 1967, Peter was appointed

Director of the Toc H hostel on Tower Hill in London. He interacted with the hostel residents and became acquainted with a group of twenty foreign students from the Sylhet district, then known as East Pakistan and since 1971 known as Bangladesh. The hostel operated as the local community center. Every Sunday, more than one hundred community workers and young people would gather in an atmosphere of friendship and discussion, including the Bangladeshis. Peter discovered a unique sense of life through these boys and at the age of sixty decided to move to Bangladesh. His friends wanted to know exactly, "What are you going to do there?" The truth was, Peter didn't know. He was simply going to live amongst his new friends. Once there, Peter saw opportunities to help others help themselves. He knew it was in doing small things that big things could happen. One of the first things he did was purchase a bike for a young man who was the bread winner of his family and who spent most of his meager wages getting to and from work. The bike not only gave this young man a means of transportation, it gave him self-respect, plus the money previously spent on transportation could now be spent on food.

The Pakistani government paid for the teachers in the public schools, however, each community had to provide their own building. In Khasdobir, where Peter lived, the existing building had room for 700 children with a waiting list of 300. The community could only raise one third of the cost needed to expand the building by adding a second story. They asked Peter if Toc H might be able to help. Peter asked, and Toc H raised the necessary funds. By the time the school was completed in 1985, it had space for 1,400 children and also served as the community social center.

Peter helped establish the Khasdobir Youth Action Group which went on to rebuild over 100 flood damaged homes and established a clothing workshop for women where they learned the trade of making clothes. Peter assisted a widow with five children by building her a home and giving her money to start a small business making baskets and mats from bamboo. Not only were people learning a skill to earn a living, in doing so, they grew in self-reliance. When Peter walked down the streets everyone called him "Peter bhai" which meant "Brother Peter."

Peter lived in Bangladesh for four years. After he returned home to England, a London teacher who visited Khasdobir said she could tell by the children where Peter had been. Throughout Bangladesh most children stood a ways off—shy—with unassuming eyes turned towards the ground. But where Peter had been, the children were welcoming, self-confident and friendly. Peter had accomplished something which might have been less obvious to the casual eye. Peter, in his quiet, friendly manner had helped change lives and attitudes.

In 1978 Toc H founded a school in Kochi, India with an enrollment of 2,300 and classes for students from kindergarten through high school. The school focuses on academic excellence along with the cultural, emotional and personal empowerment of the students. The campus of six and a half acres is fully equipped with 69,000 square feet of class rooms, an auditorium, a football field and basketball courts.

During the summer months of 1989, sixty-two programs were sponsored and run by Toc H, bringing together a remarkably diverse group of people. It was not untypical to find a variety of volunteers such as two young men recently released from prison and on probation, two British rail employees (one a manager and the other a guard with a rail strike occurring at the time), a disabled woman working as a clerical assistant, the Director of an AIDS clinic, two sixteen-year-old Asian girls and a fifty-year-old Toc H leader—all working together on weekends to perform supervised community services. Afterwards, they'd get back together and discuss what the experience meant to them.

Peter Ranken, an architect in East London had more questions than answers. He was not particularly religious and thought, "The only thoughts which really make sense are those which are grounded in your own experience." Peter volunteered to go to South Africa during the Apartheid era. As a Group Leader he led activities for children and the disabled along with doing manual labor at the Toc H Center. Peter had a powerful experience with a group of children from South Africa's largest impoverished black township outside of Johannesburg: Soweto. One day during lunch, one of the girls approached Peter and asked if she could lead. Peter agreed. Before he knew it, all the whites and blacks were singing, dancing and playing games organized by the children. They sang in Zulu, Tswana and Xhosa. It was within those magic moments Peter discovered those children, whose lives were so poor and deprived, yet were filled with joy and community spirit. Peter discovered, "As an approach to life, making sense of life and these magic moments, this means a lot. Let go, don't worry about it too much, just let it happen." During that nine-month experience, Peter became convinced about the importance of continuing to search for a meaning to his life saying, "You have to try to be aware of what happens to you. And there are things which can only be explained in a religious way, which seems to fit in with your concept of the spiritual side of a living presence, or a loving being—in fact it's very much tied up with that. The good things are connected with love, and there's something religious to that."

Toc H planted seeds in people. Projects focused on gathering a diversity of people, taking them out of their comfort zone, turning their experience into an adventure, then promoting discussion for people to talk and listen in hopes of gaining a greater, even different perspective; to think about what they were seeing, what they were doing and what they were feeling. Volunteers thought about others on this adventure with them; who they were and what were their differences? And in doing so, many learned, when you got right down to it, they weren't so different after all.

Volunteers went on to establish projects and organizations that flowed from their experience. Wayne Kistner, a young seminarian student from California became a Winant Volunteer and then went on to live in England and become a long-term Toc H volunteer. Afterwards, he returned to California and was able to obtain a Toc H grant which founded a local community outreach program named Community Concern and a Toc H adventure program called "Project Mexico." Project Mexico took groups of college students and young adult volunteers for weekend trips to one of the poorest areas of Mexico and worked with orphans. Afterwards, in the Toc H tradition, they would get together and talk about their experience of helping others.

The spirit of Talbot House continued with Toc H becoming a well spring of diversified social services. They founded the British blood transfusion service, British eye banks, hospital broadcasting networks, organized work projects to reconstruct and repair the aging canal system, built playgrounds in underprivileged neighborhoods, visited and cared for the elderly and disabled—even took them on vacations developed inner-city play programs, pioneered social services for the mentally ill, educated Gypsy children, formed a Junior Farmers Movement for children, camping programs for underprivileged children, developed youth leadership training programs, operated soup kitchens and overnight shelters for the homeless, provided clothing and food for the needy, acted as a national employment agency, provided services for drug addicts and counseled the depressed.

As one Toc H volunteer put it so distinctly, "Service to others is the rent we pay for our room on earth" or as Tubby would state, "Life is not a mere struggle for existence; it is a struggle for the life of others." Then there was Jeannie Deans an English woman who when addressing one of the Grand Dames of her time said: "Ah, Milady, when it comes to the end, it will na be the things ya ha' dune for yaisel', but the things ye ha' done for ithers that ye will think on most pleasantly."

Churches often grow old, dogmatic, ceremonial, and can, over time, lose the spiritual connection to the heart and soul of their parishioners. Guilt and "Fear of the Lord" in the 19th and 20th centuries worked. However, in the computerized era of the 21st century, people are bombarded by rapid-fire information and technical innovations which have reduced their attention spans. People need to feel alive in their faith and worship. They need to be connected. If the church goer is only an occupant of a church pew on Sundays, Christmas and Easter, so much is lost with such a stationary audience. Faith needs to be experienced for it to be real. Churches should encourage and provide members with opportunities to experience their faith, to step out and let God work within and through them. All too often, tradition, rules, bureaucracy, hierarchy and repetition make it difficult for churches to step out of their comfort zones. Churches should be wellsprings of extroverted actions towards others and not just for their selected few. For without the outward action there can be no inward calling. And for any church to do this effectively and successfully, it is necessary to have active and vibrant activities for the youth of their communities.

Was Toc H a Church? No. Was Toc H part of the Church of England? Yes. Did Tubby's actions create controversy within the hierarchy of the Anglican Church? Yes, and there were those who grew tired of Tubby, an ordained Anglican Minister, a living legend from the trenches of the Western Front, the Founder of Toc H, the

Deacon of All Hallows, the Spiritual Advisor to the King and Queen, a poet and an author.

Tubby maintained Toc H must never sit on the fence. It must move forward, asserting its Christian inspiration and openness to all. The Anglican Church went along with Tubby's assertion regarding Christian inspiration, but "openness to all?" What if they weren't Christians? Tubby wasn't an evangelist in word, he was a doer of the Word who embraced diversity in hopes of winning people over to Christ. Tubby wrote, "Any form of religion which tends to produce introverts cannot hope to command a very wide allegiance among a race of men whose ideals march with the extrovert. I am here to teach the Church that men have minds, and those minds are hungering and thirsting. Men cannot really lift their hearts to God unless their minds are also lifted up. Our Lord was not alarmed by men with minds. He never trusted cleverness per se; but he had every use for honest thinking." Tubby criticized the actions of ministers by saying, "Actors, if they succeed, make fiction appear true. But ministers of religion, if they fail, tend to make truth seem like fiction. Each should assist the other; and actors can scarcely be blamed for laxity in Churchgoing, if clergy never go to the theater."

Movements need leaders and when the leader of a movement dies, that movement struggles with its identification and future direction. When Tubby grew older, he did slow down, and Toc H continued without Tubby at the helm. It was during this time the Toc H Christian perspective was marginalized and the Movement began to distance itself from the very spiritual foundation which set it in motion. Toc H continued to celebrate the meeting of people from different walks of life, cultures and religions. Time and age finally caught up with the irascible Tubby Clayton and his earthly fire did burn out, just after his 87th birthday on December 16, 1972. Tubby was cremated. His ashes are interred in the Crypt Chapel of All Hallows. His effigy is located between the Nave and North Aisle of the Main Church, and a Toc H Lamp is seated on an altar within the Church.

The emphasis devoted to the Christian perspective was reviewed. The last thing Toc H wanted to do was to alienate others including those of different religions.

Toc H continued to provide meaningful services. In 1978, Satish Visavadia met Toc H through his physically handicapped sister who was attending a special school. He was invited to a disco at the school sponsored by young people who called themselves the Impact Group of Toc H. Satish realized, "There for the first time I saw fellowship between black and white... It was really good." Satish got involved with Toc H and said it made him, for the first time, proud of his Asian culture and it helped him discover his identity as a black Briton.

Tubby trusted men and saw them as his stepping stones to his most important relationship, his relationship with the Almighty. He was an old fashion kind of man who believed dreams could come true. He dreamed of brotherhood and the gathering of hope and faith. His dream not only survived the devastation of two World Wars, it went on to thrive and continues to this day in a modified form. In his book, Talbot House to Tower Hill, Tubby wrote, "Indeed our Lord is joy. When he rejoiced in spirit, His Father did not turn away from Him, but in Him was well pleased. Compassed about with sadness and undergoing voluntarily and deliberately every imaginable circumstance which can embitter or breed cynicism, Our Lord declined to disbelieve in men's good nature or their aptitude for recognizing virtue when they saw it. He staked His life and lost it in long drawn agony. Men broke His heart, but He continued to believe in them. He vested His whole faith in God and in His disciples."

Although much of their membership is older, the order of the day continues to be guided by the four points of the original Toc H compass: Fellowship (To Love Widely), Service (To Build Bravely); Fairmindedness (To Think Fairly); and the Kingdom of God (To Witness Humbly). Toc H supports the Winant-Clayton Volunteers and the associated Friends of Khasdobir. Although they are a Christian based movement they welcome others of no religion and those from different religions. Toc H promotes Christianity through service to others and not by preaching. They continue to be a worldwide movement with branches and members in the UK, Australia, Belgium, India, Zimbabwe, South Africa, Gibraltar, France and the United States.

PART II

Chapter Four

Wayne, C. J. & Toc H

"The finest friendships are literally an influence, for one life flows into the other, guiding it and strengthening it at every turn." Tubby Clayton

When Wayne Kistner was in the 6th grade growing up in California, during the heat of battle of a boys-will-be-boys water balloon fight, he ran through a plate glass window and severed the tendons under his knee; filleting his knee cap which flopped over. His head and his hands were cut, and he was bleeding profusely. The ambulance arrived, and he was rushed into emergency surgery. Just before surgery he pleaded with the surgeon, "Please don't cut off my leg." After four and a half hours of surgery the surgeon was able to stitch the tendons together and place Wayne's knee cap back into position. Post surgically and with the fear of infection, Wayne spent two and a half weeks in the hospital, then two and a half weeks bedridden and in a wheel chair at home. He had a full leg cast from his foot to his hip and used crutches for months. When he was first allowed to go out of the house, he hobbled over to San Mateo Central Park and noticed a group of boys surrounding a tall, distinguished looking man in a three-piece suit. This aroused Wayne's curiosity and he crutched over to check it out.

The man was engaging the boys in games and rewarding them with dollar bills. "Alright boys, everyone form a good straight and proper line. We're going to have a contest and determine just which one of you has the greatest broad jump. That's it, make it nice and straight. Alright now, when I say 'Jump' you must all jump and stop wherever you land. And there can be no moving forward after you've landed, that wouldn't be fair now would it? Alright now, on the count of three; 'one, two, three - Jump!' Well done, well done! Alright, what's your name? Very good Tommy and here is your prize (a dollar bill). And let me see here and just who might you be? ...I see. And how old are you? Ten! Well, that was a fine looking jump for a ten-year-old. Well done! Well done! And here is your prize (another dollar). You all did very well and are some of the finest broad jumpers I've ever seen."

Wayne watched with great interest and disappointment as he would have liked to compete. The man gathered everyone around him and asked, "Can anyone here tell me the date of President Abraham Lincoln's birthday?"

A voice spoke up, "I know the answer to that one mister, it's February 12th."

"Yes. Very good! And just what is your name my boy?" "Wayne, Wayne Kistner, sir."

"Well, here's your prize Mr. Kistner and I'll wager you probably don't have any idea as to what Abraham Lincoln and I have in common."

Wayne shook his head and answered, "No, I don't. What is it?"

"Well, President Lincoln was the greatest President that ever lived, he's one of the people who I admire most and, we both share the same birthday."

One of the other kids asked, "Did you know President Lincoln?"

The man laughed, "Oh no, I didn't know President Lincoln, although I certainly would have liked to, but I have known quite a few presidents in my day... yes indeed, I have."

The man held court. He was different. He was believable. He was in his seventies and wasn't like anyone Wayne had ever met; it was almost like he was from a different world. Not only was the man captivating the attention of all the boys around him, he was thoroughly enjoying himself. At the end of the games, the man handed out dollar bills to everyone then said he needed to get back to his hotel and rest, but while he was in town visiting family, he enjoyed his daily strolls through the park and would be back.

The following day the man was back, and Wayne was waiting for him. Again, the man held court, and again, Wayne participated. This time though, after the man finished and moved on, Wayne followed. "Hey mister, Hey mister, slow down, wait a minute." Wayne struggled to catch up with the gentleman who stopped and waited for him. Wayne asked, "Who are you?"

The man responded, "Well, my boy, my name is Coleman Jennings but my friends call me C.J. Would you like to call me C.J.?"

Wayne responded, "Sure!"

C.J. asked Wayne how he injured his leg and Wayne told him. C.J. told Wayne they had something in common because he recently suffered from a heart attack and had to take things easy. And so began the special friendship between a twelve-year-old Wayne Kistner and a seventy-four-year-old man of the world. When their friendship progressed, C.J. insisted he meet Wayne's parents and family. Wayne's mom, Inez, invited C.J. to join the family for home cooked meals and as C.J. became a part of Wayne's family, he'd take them out for meals.

C.J. travelled from his home in Washington, D.C. to California three to four times per year to visit his only sibling, Katherine, along with other relatives including two grand aunts. When C.J. visited California, he'd stay at the Benjamin Franklin Hotel in San Mateo. It was close to his sister who lived just blocks away in Burlingame. During his stay he'd take daily strolls in the park, rent a car and visit his aunts in San Francisco.

Wayne and C.J. would meet for walks together in the park. Wayne joined C.J. for many meals at restaurants and coffee shops and C.J. took Wayne on outings to the ocean, the zoo, trips to San Francisco, the Santa Cruz Boardwalk and often, C.J. had Wayne's family and friends accompany them. C.J. knew no boundaries to his age and could be a kid at heart, horsing around with the young Wayne. Even as an elderly stately man, C.J. and Wayne playfully boxed with each other and Wayne was surprised at how quick and agile this old guy really was. Mostly though, what Wayne and C.J. did was talk. C.J. wanted to know everything about Wayne; how he was doing in school, he wanted to see his report card and rewarded him financially for As and Bs. C.J. asked how things were at home, what interested him, who his friends were and what their activities were.

During one of their visits, C.J. took Wayne to a soda fountain and bought him an ice cream sundae. C.J. put his newspaper down on the table. Wayne picked it up and looked through *The London Times*. On page two, Wayne saw a photograph of C.J. with the byline, "American Philanthropist Receives Humanitarian Award from Queen Mother." Wayne asked C.J. what a philanthropist was and C.J. told him it's what he was; one who devoted their life to worthy causes and others. Wayne asked if he knew the Queen of England. C.J. responded he was well acquainted with the Royal Family and regarded the Queen Mother as a great friend, and during his trips to England and Scotland in the summer, he would visit with her at her royal residence, Clarence House in Westminster.

C.J.'s hotel was a short distance from Wayne's school, St. Matthew's Elementary School. Sometimes, C.J. came over during the lunch hour, met Wayne and took him and some of his friends out for lunch at a nearby restaurant. On one of those occasions, one of the boys mentioned the lunch to his mother who called the school principal and complained. She wanted to know, "…Just who is this strange man who took my son out to lunch?" The school principal, Sister Mary Leo, phoned Wayne's mother and inquired about the man. Inez told Sister Mary Leo that Mr. Jennings was a friend of the family, and a person of outstanding integrity. However, because of the mother's complaint, the principal felt she needed to inform the police, which she did, and the police stepped in to investigate.

The police contacted Mr. Jennings at his hotel and questioned him. After they concluded their investigation and realized who Mr. Jennings was, the police were completely satisfied Mr. Jennings actions and motives were filled with nothing but good intentions for those young boys. C.J. then contacted the principal who invited him for tea in her home at the convent. As the visit came to an end, Sister Mary Leo got up, thanked him for coming over and meeting with her and when Coleman Jennings departed, she graciously added, "God Bless you and the wonderful work you are doing."

C.J. had spent much of his life with youth groups, had started a club of his own for youth in Edinburgh, Scotland, worked with Toc H   and Tubby Clayton, the YMCA, the Boys Club and he would not allow any false impressions of what others thought of his well-intended actions—in any way—change what his life's work was about, and rather than avoiding inquiries such as this, he invited them. He won over the police and the school principal, and there was no further suggestion of any impropriety. To the contrary, as they understood Coleman Jennings, "C.J." was a unique and dedicated Christian whose life's work was about helping others.

Wayne cherished his relationship with his unique friend and started a C.J. Club. He introduced his friends to C.J. who took them out for meals, stimulated discussions and sponsored club activities. As Wayne and C.J.'s relationship grew, C.J. invited Wayne—at C.J.'s expense—to fly to Washington, D.C. and visit him at his home in the nation's capital. Wayne was thrilled, and his parents gave him permission to go. Upon his arrival, when Wayne exited the aircraft, C.J. greeted him and escorted Wayne to his chauffeured Cadillac.

C.J.'s home was a stately mansion located in the heart of one of the oldest and most exclusive neighborhoods in Washington, D.C. just off Embassy Row. His back yard was adjacent to the backyard of the Russian Embassy and Senator Ted Kennedy lived   two   doors over. At that time, C.J.'s home and D.C. life had been scaled back from when it had been one of the social centers of the nation's capital. When Wayne first visited, C.J. had a full-time chauffer; Dawson, who had a room at C. J.'s home, along with a full-time cook and two full-time, live-in housemaids; Mary and Dora. C.J. also had a full-time personal secretary, Bob Grimm, who devoted his life to him for forty-six years.

Wayne was escorted to his bedroom with his own private bath and enjoyed dining with C.J. in the dining room where two magnificent oil paintings of C.J.'s father and mother were proudly displayed. Dinner was served by Mary, and the cook would come out to make sure everything was prepared satisfactorily. After dinner, they'd retire into C.J.'s study—a proper gentleman's study—with floor to   ceiling bookcases, a beautiful marble fireplace, two leather lounge chairs and C.J.'s work desk. The walls of the room were adorned with black and white photos of C.J.'s family, U.S. Presidents and friends. Above the   fireplace,   hung   an   oil   painting   of a narrow-gauge train travelling across the African plains. The time spent in the study was Wayne's favorite and here they'd discuss all matters of life, religion, history and what lay ahead. Sometimes they would be in deep discussion well past midnight.

Wayne had been profoundly impacted by C.J. and in his own way had come to wanting to help others. During high school, Wayne volunteered for the Amigos de las Americas program and was sponsored by Coleman Jennings. He would spend the summer in Nicaragua working with the poor. Wayne had never travelled outside of the United States before. He went through a brief training program, learned of the high infant mortality rate and where the average life expectancy for a man was just thirty-eight years. Wayne's job was to administer vaccines for polio and smallpox, conduct basic hygiene and sanitation clinics, render basic first aid for cuts and wounds, and to build the first outhouse in the village. Before Wayne left, C.J. gave him a journal to keep during his trip. When he arrived at the impoverished village outside of Leon, there was no running water, no electricity, no motorized vehicles, and no sanitation facilities—not even a latrine. A local peasant farm family cooked Wayne and his partner's food which was unlike anything Wayne had eaten before. Wayne thought the poverty was "almost unbelievable."

During one of their clinics, a woman came in with four children and a very sick baby in her arms. Wayne conducted the pre-screening procedures and administered vaccines to her four older children. Then the mother handed Wayne her baby who Wayne thought was about three months old, although the malnourished child was more than a year. The child was suffering from a high fever and Wayne could not administer any vaccinations. The mother didn't understand and was insistent Wayne give her baby daughter medicine. As Wayne held the baby, the infant went into convulsions and died in his arms. Wayne became angry with the woman because the baby was so obviously malnourished and shouted at her in English. The woman cried and told Wayne's partner who spoke Spanish, she had many children and not enough food for all of them and her baby went hungry. Wayne was deeply upset by the experience.

Before he returned home, Wayne came down with a kidney infection and lost 20 lbs. Reflecting on his trip, Wayne said, "It was a lot for me to handle at that age, a lot for me to absorb and understand."

Yet, he found the village people warm-hearted, friendly and extremely generous with the little they had. It was during that summer Wayne made the decision that after high school he was going to enter the seminary and pursue a calling to become a priest.

When Wayne returned, C.J. read his journal and was concerned about Wayne's experience with the child dying in his arms. C.J. comforted Wayne when they spoke of it. Wayne told C.J. about his decision to enter the seminary after graduation which led to another discussion about what Wayne would be doing before entering the seminary. C.J. told Wayne about a program called the Winant - Clayton Volunteer Exchange Program which was part of a larger organization known as Toc H. C.J. explained how during the summer, American students went to England and English students came to America to perform various social work activities. C.J. said he sponsored college students, mainly from the east coast, to be part of this exciting program that started in 1948 and how he was friends with the founders: John Winant the former American Ambassador to Great Britain and a Church of England Padre by the name of Tubby Clayton. C.J. asked Wayne if he might be interested in such an opportunity. Wayne was definitely interested.

Wayne went to England expecting to be working with underprivileged and disadvantaged youth; however, his initial assignment was through a third party social service organization called "Care of the Elderly." Wayne's job was to visit shut-ins; the elderly who were unable to leave their homes. Wayne visited with them, delivered books, asked if they needed anything and went grocery shopping for them. Wayne spoke with his Winant Supervisor and communicated he had hoped to work with disadvantage youth. During his last four weeks, Wayne was reassigned to Youth Project Leadership and worked with underprivileged youth.

Each year the Queen Mother hosted a cocktail reception at Clarence House for Winant Volunteers and Tubby Clayton always attended. During the reception, Wayne was introduced to both the Queen Mother and Tubby. When Wayne met Tubby, Wayne told Tubby they shared a mutual friend in Coleman Jennings. Tubby's response, "Ah, Coleman Jennings, a Saint of a man, a Saint of a man."

Wayne returned from England and C.J. accompanied him to St. Patrick's College Seminary where one hundred twenty seminarians were enrolled. Wayne received his room assignment and together, he and C.J. met some of the other students. During his first year at the seminary, Wayne would continue to correspond regularly with C.J., visit him whenever he came to California and fly back to C.J.'s home for his annual visit.

Wayne defined their relationship saying, "C.J. was more than a grandfather figure to me, he was more of a mentor, a friend, an advisor and in many ways, I was closer to him than I was my own father. There wasn't any important decision that I was making in my life from the time that I got back from Nicaragua; there wasn't any decision or direction that my life took that wasn't shared with him and that he wasn't a major part of."

When asked if C.J. was trying to guide his life Wayne answered, "In a very real way he was guiding my life, whether he was trying to or not, he was. I very much respected him, valued and loved him and I felt that he loved me and so it was a great, great person to have in my life during that period of time, because I absolutely trusted him. I was still confused and trying to sort out what I wanted to do, to have someone of his age and wisdom to care about me, making those choices was an incredible experience for me and he never steered me the wrong way."

When asked about his faith C.J. said, "Sometimes I thought that perhaps I wouldn't be the most helpful person in this area of religion because I was just a very lucky person and God gave me an extraordinary simple faith in him. When my dear parents taught me to say my little prayers, I felt I was praying to a God that was very real and I just had the vastly good fortune to have faith in Him all my life. But the people I admire most in this religious field are those who have not had such an easy time as me, who've had to struggle with their religious faith and had to work about it, think about it... study it. But to be honest with you, you've asked me a question that I can answer frankly, that from the very smallest childhood I had the most joyous confidence in God."

When C.J. was asked who God was he answered, "I will have absolutely nothing to contribute in that area except to say what is God like to me, and I can answer that. My absolute center of all my religious thinking is Jesus Christ. What was God to Jesus Christ? He was his loving father and he absolutely felt that God was the center of all his living, his thinking, his decisions and everything and therefore, I accept Christ's view of God and I think He's my Loving Father."

During his first year in the seminary Wayne was uncertain about whether he wanted to devote his life to being a priest. He reinitiated contact with Toc H and along with input from C.J., Toc H extended an invitation for him to return to England for a year of service as a Long-Term Volunteer. It wasn't a salaried position, but Toc H would pay for Wayne's room and board and give him spending money. One of the attractive aspects of the position: he'd be treated the same as paid staff and would attend conferences and meetings. Wayne needed a break to re-evaluate his passion to become a priest. He packed his bags, flew over the pond and was back in England.

He was assigned to the Toc H Midlands headquarters in Birmingham and moved into Toc H Mark #6, a four story Victorian mansion located in the small village of Mosley, just outside the Birmingham City Center. Wayne's supervisor was John Mitchell who assigned him to different activities including the Birmingham Soup Kitchen, and working in the crypt at St. Chad's Cathedral handing out pillows and blankets to the homeless as they came into the shelter for a night off the streets. He worked on youth projects and Adventure Playgrounds that were part of an international movement to build unique playgrounds in inner cities where pre-teen kids were given the opportunity to freely build and construct whatever they wanted. The land was donated by the city and Toc H supplied volunteers along with youth leadership to oversee this creative endeavor. Wayne became a member of the West Midlands Gypsy Liaison sponsored by Toc H; an eclectic group of well-intentioned teachers, college students, social workers and ministers. They were a controversial social action group and frowned upon, even within the ranks of Toc H because they worked with Gypsies. This Gypsy Liaison group would watch-dog Gypsy evictions to ensure both the police and bailiffs followed the laws; which often they did not. Wayne became a predominant activist within the group and was often in the media including the newspapers, radio and the BBC.

Wayne was assigned a group of twenty students including high school girls, borstal boys (juvenile delinquents) and students from Birmingham University. It was all done in the spirit of Toc H; the spirit of Tubby Clayton, in faith and in trust. He set up living quarters in a community hall, divided them into small groups and during the day worked at building Adventure Playgrounds. They hunted for building materials along roadsides and junkyards, worked with the kids digging tunnels, hanging swings, building ladders going nowhere, a basketball hoop with an old tire for a rim, pounded stuff together and called it art. In the evenings they'd cook meals together, pack lunches for the next day and have group discussions.

When Wayne's Long-Term Volunteer program with Toc H ended, he decided not to return to the seminary and returned to Southern California where he moved back home with his parents, found a job and started attending the local community college. However, he now had a vision because of his Toc H experience. He wanted to develop a program with service projects where the focus of youth service activities would be based on the principles and philosophy of Toc H. Wayne discussed his vision with C.J. who completely supported it and referred to it as a "Great Project."

Wayne organized a group of faculty from Cypress College and other community leaders and drafted a proposal for a program based on Toc H principles. He returned to London and presented the proposal to the Board of Directors for Toc H. C.J. wrote Wayne, "...your desire to make a real contribution through your Toc H experience and plant a seed in the United States may produce a vigorous, but perhaps different kind of flower. I shall eagerly be awaiting your next letter to hear of Toc H's decision. How I hope it will be favorable."

Not only did C.J. support Wayne, he used his influence and lobbied for Wayne by personally writing to John Mitchell and other key people of Toc H:

> "Toc H has played a very big role in my life since I first heard of it in about 1924. I started the Washington Branch of Toc H, of which I was Chairman during its existence from 1925 to 1935. Our Branch was recognized as a 'Mark,' and given the Lamp. I later became Chairman of the Toc H Movement in the U.S., which had branches in New York, Philadelphia, Baltimore, and Boston, as well as Washington, D.C.

> One of the great blessings that came to me during this period, and by annual trips to England, and visits

from Tubby to my home, was the deep friendship which I established with him...

Though the active work of Toc H only lasted about ten years in this country, it left an enduring impression on many of its members and friends, including several clergy who were associated with it. The seeds that were planted during these years influenced many lives... it is my firm faith in the basic principles of Toc H and in the enormous influence it has had in Great Britain and in other parts of the world... This brings me to Wayne Kistner, whom I introduced to Toc H, and who has since shared with me his reactions to his experiences and his dreams for the future... I want you to know of my total backing of Wayne's general concepts he has outlined for you... I have great faith in my young friend, who in my opinion has unusual qualities of leadership, and has become inspired to channel his energies into a life of service... He has great hopes to translate the methods of Toc H into a workable program for Volunteers in this country... It might be a valuable extension of Toc H, sparking a movement in this country built upon the great discoveries which Toc H has made."

Toc H approved Wayne's proposal and funded it with a $15,000 grant in 1975, along with Wayne receiving additional financial assistance from C.J. Fifteen thousand dollars back then was a lot of money. Wayne named the program "Community Concern," established it in the city of Cypress and developed "Project Mexico," a Toc H type project where college students went to Mexico and worked at an orphanage in Tijuana known as the Tijuana Christian Mission (TCM). Project Mexico would caravan groups of twelve to twenty students in vans down to TCM. The orphanage was an ongoing construction project and there was always work to be done. College students spent weekends doing cement and brickwork, repairs, removing garbage, painting and they'd play with the kids which was the best part of the trip. It gave volunteer students a weekend providing service in a Third World country and included group discussions of how the experience impacted them. Students were shocked to see such poverty, as most had never seen the poor on such a scale. It was all taken directly from the Toc H manual, including the after-project discussions called "Debriefings," a term Tubby had picked up from the trenches.

Community Concern continued to develop, and a second branch was opened at the University of California at Irvine which also included Project Mexico.

The first Project Mexico trip began in the summer of 1975. During Wayne's time at the orphanage, the Orphanage Director invited him to make a garbage run to the Tijuana Dump, saying he wanted to show him something. They loaded the truck with bags of garbage and off they went. In the middle of the Tijuana Dump was a village where people lived in cardboard, crudely constructed shacks or under tarps connected to the garbage. There was a stream of filthy, brown water which they drank from. There were no sanitation facilities. The people living here were illegal squatters and literally living off the trash of others. Part of the Director's ministry was to check on the children at the dump and whatever was left of their families. Many of the kids were orphans and sometimes the Director would bring them back to TCM. That's what the Director wanted Wayne to see; the children and the hopeless poverty of the Tijuana Dump.

Coleman Jennings died in 1978. He was the first president of the Washington Community Chest which became the United Way. He was a trustee of the Boys' Club the predecessor to the Boys and Girls Club, Charity Chief and Chairman of the Service Commission of the Federation of Churches. He received an award from the Washington Federation of Churches for his assistance in "every Christian enterprise" and for his "splendid record" of service. He was a man who devoted his life and resources to developing relationships and service towards others.

Wayne merged Community Concern with an established social service program called Straight Talk Clinic and became the Executive Director. Project Mexico continued for years and Straight Talk Clinic remains in operation to this day. Wayne went on to law school, got married and started a family. He became a partner in a law firm and continues to involve himself in community service.

Chapter Five

Amor Ministries – How It All Began

"Come down and change lives! Come down and have your life changed!" Scott Congdon

Rooted in the trenches of World War I, Tubby Clayton, Talbot House and Toc H, and from those seeds planted within Community Concern and Project Mexico, a new movement would spring forth.

Scott Congdon was born in 1956 a Navy Brat. His father, Robert Congdon graduated from Annapolis Naval Academy and served as a Captain during much of his career. Captain Congdon served in both the Korean and Vietnam Wars and was away from home up to nine months at a time, especially from 1972-75 during the Vietnam War. He was awarded the Legion of Merit, two Commendation Medals and the Bronze Star for exceptional meritorious conduct, bravery and heroism during combat. Scott's mom, Colleen is a cultured woman and a homemaker. She graduated from University of California Berkley, is an accomplished pianist, singer, and loves to paint people and nature with water colors and oils, and volunteers as a docent at the San Diego Museum. Scott has one younger brother, Craig. The Congdon family moved often transferring to different naval bases about every three years. Scott attended junior high in Virginia when his father served in the Pentagon. While in Vietnam and before his retirement, Scott's father was promoted to Commodore and commanded a fleet of ships from San Diego where Scott attended and graduated from Patrick Henry High School.

Scott's father was not a churchgoing man or a Christian; however, he believed in many of the values and characteristics of the Christian faith. On occasion, while living in San Diego, Colleen would take her sons to the Presbyterian Church but for the most part, the Congdon family was not religious or a church going family. Scott's dad died in 2015.

Growing up, Scott loved animals. During his childhood he was always bringing stray dogs, lizards, snakes, rabbits, wounded birds and squirrels home, and his mom let him keep whatever critter he could get his hands on. In particular, Scott loved big animals and went horseback riding whenever he could. While in high school, he landed his dream job at the San Diego Zoo and Wild Animal Park, and worked closely in the animal hospital with a zoo keeper and Doctor Terry Spraker, one of the zoo's veterinarians.

Scott enrolled at the University of California Irvine (UCI) with the goal of becoming a veterinarian working with large exotic animals. Scott moved out of his home for the first time and into an on-campus co-ed dorm where suddenly, he was exposed to a different side of life with drugs, alcohol, sex and wild partying. He continued to commute home whenever he could; on weekends, holidays, Spring Break and summer, and he continued to work at the San Diego Wild Animal Park.

Scott quickly became disillusioned by what was taking place with his peers on campus versus the values and discipline he was brought up with. He wrestled with those issues. On the one hand, Scott wanted to fit in and be accepted, yet, there was deep division between how he was raised and the careless, carefree living of young students kicking up their heels while being away from home for their first time. It was during this time of confusion that Dr. Terry Spraker and the zoo keeper took a special interest in Scott and started telling him how faith in Christ made a difference in their lives. They told Scott about the Lord; who He was and how He changed them. Scott listened closely to his zoo mentors during this challenging time and found what he needed to know—that Jesus Christ is the Son of a loving God. The zoo keeper invited Scott to join him at a Sunday service at Calvary Chapel in North Park, San Diego led by Pastor Mike Macintosh. During that service in 1976, Scott Congdon accepted the Lord.

When Scott told his parents he had become a Christian it wasn't an issue, not even for his dad. Robert Congdon understood the foundation of the United States is deeply rooted in Christianity. He thought prayer should be allowed in schools and the Ten Commandments should be displayed within the court houses. Scott said, "My dad is absolutely one of the most moral men I've ever met and as a result of that, the values and the character that Christ portrays in terms of being human is very easy, because my dad raised his kids with absolute integrity. So, from that point of view, it was a good fit."

After Scott became a Christian, some college friends invited him to go down to Mexico suggesting, "Hey, we're going to Mexico with this organization called Community Concern on a trip called Project Mexico. We're going down to an orphanage and while we're in Mexico do some shopping." Scott spent much of his adolescence growing up in San Diego, with Mexico being only twenty minutes away, but he had never been, plus college students needed to stretch their dollar, and in Mexico, dollars could be stretched a long way. The invitation sounded like an adventure. Scott thought, "Shopping! That sounds cool. I heard you could get some really cheap blankets, sombreros and piñatas." Later Scott said, "I had no idea that anything was going to happen to me on that trip. I thought I was pretty much going down to enjoy myself."

When Scott arrived at the orphanage his world was rocked, and he anguished, "It ripped my heart out. I had never been to an orphanage or anywhere in the world before like that, seeing three, four children sleeping to a bed. The smells were just urine everywhere, the bathrooms and toilets were horrible. Most of their heads were shaved because of lice. But the children were so happy. At lunch time they put them all in this little dining hall with picnic tables. Everything was painted white to try to keep it clean, the rooms, the walls, the ceilings, the picnic tables. There were fifty children sitting there, very quietly, waiting for their food. The plates came out and they had just a little bit of beans, a little bit of rice and a tortilla. I'm like: 'That's it?' Then a little girl stood up on one of the benches and everybody bowed their heads, and she prayed in Spanish. I had tears streaming down my face and I'm thinking, this little girl—you could just feel the passion she had for God and the love of God—but to thank Him for this, measly little meal. You know to me as an American, it was an unsuitable amount of food for a little child. I couldn't understand it but it was just incredible. I can just see it; hear it today when I think about it. That was a first awakening... what is that faith like? What is a faith that believes to thank God for every little thing? To not be distracted and focused on all the other things. We have so many distractions in the United States. How can you be thankful for a little bit of beans, rice and a tortilla; and to be so thankful about it? Now, that's a faith I want to understand."

Scott played with the kids and said when you got to know them, "It just rocked your values and rocked your world. How can they be so happy? How can they love God so much when in our society we're told that success and happiness and contentment has to do with what we have, how much we've acquired?"

The Director of the orphanage watched Scott as he played with the kids, then came up to Scott and told him, "God has you here for a reason."

Scott exclaimed, "What?"

The Director explained, "No, I can tell. The Bible says you can see a man's soul through his eyes. Come here, I want to show you something." He took Scott to his office, opened his Bible, pointed to Isaiah 58:9-12, and said, "Here it is."

Scott read, "Then when you call, the Lord will answer. 'Yes, I am here' he will quickly reply. 'Remove the heavy yoke of oppression... Feed the hungry, and help those in trouble. Then your light will shine out from the darkness, and the darkness around you will be as bright as noon. The Lord will guide you continually, giving you water when you are dry and restoring your strength. You will be like a well-watered garden, like an ever-flowing spring. Some of you will rebuild the deserted ruins of your cities. Then you will be known as a rebuilder of walls and a restorer of homes.'"

The Director again told Scott, "God has you here for a reason and He wants to use you and you need to be open.

Scott asked, "What does that mean?"

The Director answered, "You've come a hundred miles down here for God to do something. I can see that He's doing something in your life."

Scott thought to himself, "I don't understand." But by the time Scott got into the van to leave, the seeds of Project Mexico from Tubby Clayton's universal message of faith in action had been planted. Scott remembers thinking life before Project Mexico was as a typical college kid being worried about what stereo he had, how many records he owned, who had the latest and best albums, who had the best toys, and of course—who had the coolest car. After his Project Mexico trip, Scott realized, "On that day, it never mattered again! If those kids could be so happy and have such faith without all the stuff, why am I letting this stuff, the rat race, the Jones and all that get to me? Boy, it made me realize what a fast paced, rat-race we're on to nowhere, and we don't even know it."

Scott couldn't stop thinking and talking about his experience. At the time, he was responsible for his fraternity's community outreach program and needed to come up with an activity. They had just completed an Easter Seal fund raiser and Scott thought, "If the orphanage could influence and touched my heart in such a way, imagine what a positive experience it could have on the guys." He phoned the Orphanage Director and told him, "I need to bring down my fraternity."

The Director referred Scott to Gayla Cooper, a youth minister in San Diego who worked with the orphanage and helped coordinate trips. Scott phoned Gayla, introduced himself and told her about his Community Concern trip and how he wanted to arrange a trip for his fraternity. Gayla had led numerous youth groups to the orphanage including Community Concern's Project Mexico. She had taken fraternities down and knew what raucous male college students were like and thought, "Yeah great, a guy from a fraternity, and he's bringing his fraternity guys, just great, just what the orphanage needs." But Scott insisted and wanted to follow up with Gayla to talk about how arrangements could be made. Gayla suggested, "Well, I'm going down to the orphanage next weekend, why don't you come down and meet with me?"

Scott heard something in Gayla's voice; she was from Texas and had the most beautiful southern accent. While on the phone, Scott's thinking, "Wow!" Scott didn't have a girlfriend, just lots of friends. Gayla's voice sounded wonderful, her personality on the phone was stunning and Scott thought, "I cannot wait to meet this girl." But at the end of the conversation Gayla added, "Come on down, we'll go to Mexico with my kids for the orphanage Christmas Party."

Scott's hopes were dashed, thinking, "Figures, the good ones are always married."

Scott met Gayla in front of her apartment with no pretensions or hope for romance. He asked, "So where are your kids?"

Gayla answered, "They're at the church." They got in Scott's car and drove to the church where eight kids of different sizes and colors were waiting.

A confused Scott asked, "Those are your kids?"

Gayla answered, "Yeah, they're the kids in my youth group and they're going down with us to Mexico in the church van."

Scott breathed a sigh of relief, the flame in his heart reignited and he thought, "OK, this is cool!"

They all went to the TCM Christmas party that Gayla coordinated. Santa handed out gifts to the orphans and guests included orphanage supporters. The kids were excited, and Scott played with them throughout the day. Occasionally, Scott looked over at Gayla and in her discrete and selected moments, Gayla, out of the corner of her eye, looked back at Scott. Scott thought, "Boy, is she cute," and "Wow, she loves kids, she loves disadvantaged kids."

Scott had never met anyone quite like Gayla before; not even close—someone who was more concerned about others than trying to see if she could get a date. As a matter of fact, dating wasn't even on Gayla's radar but she kept looking at Scott and he kept looking at her. They were obviously attracted to each other and little did they know, from that moment on, they would never be apart!

On the way back, Scott spoke to Gayla about how he could put a fraternity trip together. A trip that would never happen because almost overnight, Scott's values changed, and the fraternity became meaningless to him—an afterthought—and he could care less if he ever went to another frat party again.

Gayla was born in California in 1954. Bud Cooper, Gayla's dad, was in the Navy and when Gayla was just eighteen months old he retired and went to work for Gulf Oil in the oil fields of West Texas and Eastern New Mexico where the family settled in the small town of Crane, Texas. Gayla grew up a Texan, but there was something different about her from the get go. Gayla said, "I came out of the womb singing Motown, not Country and Western."

The Coopers were a tightly knit, clannish family who loved sports. Gayla had an older and younger brother. She grew up in the small

Independent Christian Church where she witnessed her parents accept Christ. When Gayla was eight years old she accepted Christ as her Savior saying, "I always knew." Bud helped build the Guadalupe Christian Service Camp in the Guadalupe Mountains between Carlsbad, New Mexico and El Paso, Texas. It was at that camp, just one year after accepting the Lord, at just nine years old when Gayla dedicated her life to being a missionary. The following year she led her next-door neighbors, a Mexican family to Christ. Gayla attributes her missionary spirit to her mother who was part Cherokee Indian and always telling people about Christ and bringing them to Church. Whenever Virginia and Bud heard there were new people in town, they were on their doorsteps welcoming them.

Surrounded and protected with brothers on both sides, Gayla became very independent and grew in confidence. Her brothers were athletes and from her earliest memory, sports made her blood boil, especially football, and especially the Dallas Cowboys.

Gayla put herself through college working in retail, first attending Arizona State and then Pacific Christian College (PCC) in Southern California which today is Hope International University. During her senior year, a friend invited Gayla to Knott's Berry Farm where she was supervising a field trip with orphans from TCM. The moment Gayla met those Mexican kids she fell in love with them.

Afterwards, Gayla's friend invited her to TCM to visit the kids at the orphanage. But Gayla, a blond toe head, like most was afraid and thought, "Mexico isn't safe. If I go, something will happen to me." Yet, Gayla wanted to see and experience those kids again. She hesitated, then said, "OK, let's go."

In her mind, Gayla promised herself she'd go just that one time. Three girls went down together and Gayla readily admits she was scared stiff, refusing to eat any Mexican food fearing it would make her sick. She ate at the border Jack-In-the-Box. Once there and once again, there was something about those kids that captured Gayla's heart. She thought about how she knew people who had everything and how these kids had nothing, yet they could be so happy. After that trip, something happened to Gayla, and despite her fears and promise to never return, Gayla has never stopped going to Mexico.

When Gayla graduated from PCC she had an epiphany and decided to live and work at the orphanage. When she moved to Mexico, her parents were disappointed, thinking that being a missionary was for other Christians, not their daughter. Her dad was most concerned and afraid for his daughter living and working in Tijuana, Mexico—a Third World country. But Gayla, a strong willed, independent, "A" type personality, gifted with the ability to go beyond other's frailties was determined not to be daunted by the challenges. She was convicted by her faith and believed this is where God was directing her.

TCM's operations were unorganized; the books were a mess and with most of the funding coming from the U.S. the orphanage needed accountability if support was going to continue. Gayla took on that responsibility, managed the books and gave the orphanage the accountability it needed. She lived at the orphanage half-time and the other half in Southern California. Along with doing the books, Gayla coordinated and promoted groups coming to TCM from Oregon, California and Arizona, including Community Concern's Project Mexico.

When Gayla and Scott first met they were young, idealistic, and the orphans of Mexico were their oyster of hope and love. Scott explained, "We knew that right where we were was the beginning and we were going to change the world."

Scott was in his senior year at UCI and well on his way to graduate school to fulfill his lifelong dream of becoming a veterinarian. He lived on campus in the only mobile home park in the California university system. It was student cheap, only $75 per month, including utilities. He had a part-time job on campus where he trained and managed forty volunteer students who led campus tours for prospective new students.

After his first trip to Mexico, Scott just couldn't "shut-up" about his experience. He literally told everyone and anyone who would listen about what he saw and what the needs were. Word spread around campus and students responded with Scott discovering piles of food and clothing in front of his office door each morning. He would arrive early in the a.m., before his boss arrived and load everything into the back of his 1972 Chevy Vega Station Wagon. When it was full, he'd phone Gayla and say, "Hey, my car's full of stuff. I'm going to come down to the orphanage." There was so much stuff showing up in front of his office, Scott made trips almost every weekend.

Scott didn't know where all the stuff was coming from. The food and clothing flowed like manna from heaven. Scott re-evaluated his college path and the direction of his life. He realized that animals are great, and he is passionate about them but thought, "How do I live and go to bed at night knowing there are babies and children who are going hungry... and I've seen them?" He prayed, "OK God, I don't understand. I'm on this path to go to graduate school, right? Why can't I get these children and their needs I saw in Mexico out of my head and what, what do you want me to do?"

Within Scott's head was the Hound of Heaven's haunting voice crying out, "God has you here for a reason."

Scott prayed to God asking, "Lord you have to show me. You have to tell me what it is that you want me to do, because I don't understand." He prayed that same prayer, every day for two weeks. Then, early one morning, Scott's boss arrived before he did and saw all the stuff stacked outside his office.

When Scott arrived, she called him into her office and asked, "What's all that garbage doing outside your door?"

Scott told her about his weekend trips to Tijuana. He explained, "It's the most amazing thing, it's not garbage. Just about every morning I come in, there are boxes of food and clothes here for this orphanage down in Mexico."

She told Scott, "Well, isn't that neat. But it's got to stop. This is not a collection point for the orphanage."

Scott replied, "That's the funny part, I don't know how to stop it. I don't know where it's coming from."

His boss repeated, "No, I'm telling you, it has to stop."

Scott thought about what she said and responded, "Well, it sounds to me like you're asking me to choose between my job or helping the orphanage."

She answered, "I guess so. I guess that's what I'm doing."

Scott answered, "WOW! You're asking me to choose between the orphanage and the kids and my job." Scott explained, "You may not understand this but I've been praying for two weeks that God would tell me what to do, show me how to make sense out of all this. And you're asking me to choose between my job and them. You just answered my prayer. God just used you to answer my prayer."

She responded, "What are you talking about?"

Scott asked, "How much notice do you need?"

She was surprised but answered, "Two weeks."

Scott quipped, "OK, you got it."

Scott says that moment was incredible because he then knew what God wanted him to do. He was elated and excited in the thrill of knowing. However, by the time he walked back to his campus trailer, another reality set in: "Oh no! What have I done? How much money was I making? What am I going to tell my parents? How am I going to buy gas to go to Mexico?"

For Scott it literally meant "leave my job and change my career." Right then and there, it was a done deal; he wasn't going to become a veterinarian and pursue his lifelong dream and ambition to work with animals. He prayed about it, God answered his prayer and he knew God wanted him to be working with orphans in Mexico. When Scott told his mom and dad—just like Gayla's parents—they were surprised, didn't understand and were disappointed saying, "What are you doing? Are you sure? Is this what you really want to do?"

During his last senior semester, serving side-by-side with Gayla, Scott continued making trips down to Mexico loaded with stuff in the back of his Chevy Vega; however, the drop-off point changed from the front of his office to the front of his campus trailer.

Soon after Scott made his decision to quit his job at the university, the Tijuana River flooded displacing 90,000 people. Scott started calling newspapers. He was impulsive and naïve, all he knew is he had to tell everybody he could about the need; just spread the word about what the needs were. Scott figured God would figure out the rest. Scott went to every radio station and newspaper he could, including the Orange County Register and the Los Angeles Times. He just walked into their offices, without an appointment and demanded, "I need to talk to someone. I've got a story to tell. There are people in Tijuana, and there's been a flood. I want to organize food and clothes and blankets and whatever we can." Pretty soon the calls were coming in like crazy. Scott rented a large U-Haul and jammed it full of needed supplies. He drove the truck down to Mexico, talked the border guards into letting him through, drove to the orphanage and distributed clothing, tents, blankets and food.

For one of his final papers, Scott conducted a Mexico Orphanage Survey and visited twenty-five orphanages in northern Baja assessing their needs. He came across an orphanage outside of Tecate in Valle de las Palmas where a family farm was housing twenty-five orphans in a rat-infested barn. He had plans drawn up and hoped one day to build an orphanage to replace the barn.

It wasn't like Scott and Gayla were dating or going through a traditional courtship, but from the moment they met, they were partners in ministry and they wanted to be in each other's company constantly. They had a mission and a purpose to being together, they had become best friends and there was that good, old fashion, boy-girl chemistry between them with electricity and sparks. Then it happened, one day in front of Gayla's church, in the car after they returned from Mexico, Scott kissed Gayla.

When the elders of Gayla's church learned the young man Gayla was seeing was working with their youth group and hadn't been baptized, they concluded he was a "heathen" or something along those lines. They told Gayla that even though she and Scott were good friends—even dating—she was unequally yoked with one who hadn't been baptized and he wasn't welcome.

Scott was a new believer and did not understand the importance of baptism. He was going to church, sitting, worshiping and leaving. Serving with Gayla at her church was his first real experience in terms of working with an organized church, and now, along with being a relatively new Christian and in love, the church elders were saying, "Get him out of here!"

Scott was devastated by this and asked, "Why would the church that follows Jesus Christ exclude people, not wanting to include them?" Scott wrestled with it, questioning why a church would do such a thing when he was passionately following Christ and passionately wanting to serve Him. Those elders never gave Scott the courtesy of sitting down and speaking with him. They just told Gayla, "He's got to go." Scott and Gayla were in love and serving Christ, and because of those elders foolish actions, Gayla resigned from her youth leadership role and left that church.

Scott's life had undergone rapid and profound changes and although he was on fire with a passion to serve, his mind and heart were in a freefall of conflict and confusion. When Scott thought about what had happened, he prayed to God saying, "I don't understand why you would allow baptism to hurt people and not include people."

His spiritual dilemma would be resolved when one of the Board of Directors of TCM, out of the blue suggested, "Hey Scott, guess what? I just want you to know how much I love you and if you ever want to be baptized I'd love to talk about it."

Scott answered, "We're leaving right now."

Stunned, his friend asked, "What are you talking about?"

Scott explained, "Hey, I've been praying about this for a long time and you're the answer to my prayer and I know that; let's do it." They drove down to the Pacific Ocean and Scott was baptized, bingo, just like that, right then and there. Sometimes, if we let it, life can work that way. Scott had been struggling and praying about baptism but he had never received an invitation to be baptized. Scott had learned, "I'm not a person to say 'No' to God. I'm impulsive if God says it and I know it—then I'm going to do it."

By the time Scott graduated from UC Irvine he was filing papers to incorporate as a non-profit and a Non-Government Organization (NGO). He and Gayla first called their non-profit "Aiding Mexican Orphans and Refugees." The refugee part originated from those who lost everything in the Tijuana Flood. Two years later, the refugee part was no longer applicable to what they were doing. The acronym for Aiding Mexican Orphans and Refugees was—amazingly—AMOR which means love in Spanish. It was perfect, and they started calling themselves Amor Ministries.

Gayla and Scott were filled with youthful enthusiasm and driven by mission and purpose; they were going to change the world by eradicating poverty, and right where they stood was where they would begin. They started by thinking and believing, "This is God's mission. There's poverty staring us in the face. We've got to eliminate it. We've got to do what we can right here, right now."

They thought, "If we could get more people down here, we can really make an impact." Scott and Gayla started mobilizing groups from all over the country and Amor started to grow. They believed all they had to do was get people down to the orphanage and watch what God does with them.

Gayla and Scott organized a fundraising dinner for TCM in Tustin, California, at a small church. The dinner was for volunteers who were supporting TCM. It was an evening to say, "Thank You," a time for everyone to get to know each other better and hopefully, raise some needed funds. Scott and Gayla's table included new volunteers. Sitting next to Scott was a young, energetic Theresa Thompson who was the secretary for Johar Industries which manufactured all the padding for BMX Bikes. Theresa had left her home when she was young and by the time she was seventeen did not have a home. The President of Johar Industries was John Shattuck, who along with his wife, Anne, took Theresa into their home and gave her a job. They didn't adopt Theresa in the formal sense but adopted her in every other way. Theresa became one of the family; they loved her, and John has been "Dad" to her ever since.

At the dinner, Theresa listened to Scott and could relate to what it was like to be an orphan. She told Scott what they were doing was "Wonderful...and hey, do you guys have an office?"

Scott answered, "Well, it's like kind of... in the back of this old trailer on the campus at the University."

She responded, "Really?" She looked at John, her adopted dad asking, "Do you think we have some office space we could give them?"

John answered, "Well sure."

Theresa looked at Scott and added, "Do you guys have like, newsletters and brochures?"

Scott answered, "I've just got this one card. I made it myself."

Again, she turned to her dad and boss and asked, "Do you think we can print stuff for them, let them use our printer and make their cards and newsletters?"

Mr. John Shattuck answered, "Yeah, yeah, we can do that."

She then asked Scott, "Do you have desks and chairs and things for an office?"

Scott told her he had an old couch at the end of his trailer.

She was incredible, unbelievable and asked John, "Do you think we can get them a phone and office equipment?"

He gladly agreed, "Sure, we can do that."

Then Theresa asked, "Do you have a truck to take stuff to Mexico?" Scott could hardly believe his ears, it was just too good to be true and answered, "Well, my 72 Chevy Vega Station Wagon, which is just barely hanging in there."

Once again, she looks at her boss and asked, "Hey, do you think we can let him use our truck?"

John answered, "Yeah, on the weekends nobody's using it. I can even give them a driver and pay for the gas. Yeah, we'd love to do that."

This dinner conversation, just like the donations Scott received at UCI was manna from heaven and, there was still more to come. John Shattuck looked at Scott and suggested, "I'll tell you what, this is my card, come up to my office and we'll talk about this some more."

The following week, Gayla and Scott were sitting in John Shattuck's office with John and Theresa discussing all the ideas from the dinner. During that conversation, Theresa chimed in once again and asked Scott and Gayla, "Do you have a secretary to answer your phone calls and do your mailings."

Scott answered, "No, it's just me and Gayla."

John suggested, "Hey Theresa, would you like to work for them if I paid you and you worked for their company?"

Theresa exclaimed, "Really!?" That day, everything they spoke of started to come to fruition and Theresa Thompson started to work for Amor Ministries.

John's generosity prompted by Theresa's actions catapulted Amor Ministries forward. John let them use his company vehicles, gave them the use of his company credit card and even paid Theresa to work for them. John Shattuck, President of Johar Industries, a loving father and a generous Christian became the benefactor that God put into Scott and Gayla's life. He was moved by the appeals of his adopted daughter, the needs of the orphanage and he acted spontaneously with a big heart and an open pocketbook. He was a Christian businessman who believed God had blessed him with a prosperous business enabling him to help others, believing the profits of Johar Industries should go to spreading the Gospel and doing missionary work. He wasn't an ordained pastor or a missionary, but in a sense, he was. He was the pastor of his company and he made sure the tools and profits of Johar were put to good use helping others. John not only supported

Amor with his daughter, pocket book, company vehicles, office space and equipment, he rolled up his sleeves and went down to Mexico with Amor and worked at the orphanage on many occasions.

Before the 1970s, there were few organized youth ministries in Christian churches. During the 1970s two youth workers in their 20s, Wayne Rice and Mike Yaconelli recognized youth ministry was the vital and critical link if churches were going to grow with vitality and remain strong. Mike and Wayne concluded there was an absolute need for connecting and directing the incredible energy of teenagers to the Christian truth found within churches. They were unique, and it was said that putting the dynamic energy and personalities of Wayne and Mike together was like "turning a pharmacy over to drug addicts." They were convinced they could make it fun, rewarding and exciting, and wrote books called "Ideas Books," instructing youth leaders how to organize youth activities.

They were like magic, stimulating and promoting youth ministry when it was sorely needed. The unique actions of these two—off-the-wall—Christian leaders pioneered the movement of youth leadership with organized, and sometimes crazy ideas and activities, attracting teenagers into churches throughout the United States. They called it Youth Specialties (YS) and kicked off the first National Youth Workers Convention in 1970. YS grew and by the mid-1980s had spread across the country producing three annual conventions covering the East Coast, the Midwest and the West Coast while drawing up to 30,000 youth pastors and attendees each year.

In 1980, YS held their National Youth Workers Convention in Portland, Oregon and Amor attended as an Exhibitor promoting Mission Trips to Mexico. Taking youth down to Mexico was the last place in the world churches and parents were thinking of sending their kids. TCM had been a pioneer in marketing youth mission trips to churches. When Scott first visited TCM there were six churches along with Community Concern's Project Mexico bringing groups down from California, and those were all cutting edge groups. Nobody was doing anything like that in those days. Scott and Gayla took that idea to the largest youth ministry convention in the country.

John Shattuck loaned them his company station wagon and off they drove on the 2,200-mile round trip. Scott built a small booth, Gayla hung photos of the orphans and orphanage. Scott even painted a rainbow. There were about three hundred youth workers attending with fifty exhibitors at the small trade show. Amor was the only one promoting youth mission trips. They attracted the attention of just one person, College and Career Pastor, Le Spivey from the Evangelical Free Church of Johnson Heights in Surrey, British Columbia, Canada.

As a result, Pastor Spivey, along with thirty-six college students and young adults from EV Free, charted a bus for the 3,600-mile round trip and would be the first Amor group to go down to Mexico and start building Amor's first orphanage with construction beginning in 1981. They met Scott at a hotel in San Diego and the next day followed him to the Valle de las Palmas orphanage. There Scott gave them his plans he had drawn up to replace the rat-infested barn.

When they arrived at the farm, Scott already had the field staked with little flags marking the dimensions of the building. It was about 5,000 square feet. Scott directed the young Canadians, "OK, there's the corners of the building, here's the plans, there's the sand, there's the cement, there's the blocks, the hardware store is about twenty miles that way, the grocery store is ten miles that way and the Orphanage Director kind-of speaks some English if you need help. Gayla and I will be back to take you out in a week."

Scott and Gayla had accomplished much of their purpose which was to connect EV Free to the orphanage, rely on them to bring what money they could, follow the plans Scott had drawn up and begin building the orphanage. Scott and Gayla couldn't stay during the week as they worked at TCM where Scott now sat on the Board of Directors.

Just as Scott and Gayla were about to leave, Pastor Spivey went into a panic saying, "I can't find my briefcase! I think I left it in the hotel lobby in San Diego!" He told Scott he packed all their passports, ID's and all their money in that briefcase, more than $3,000 in cash to pay for everything: the bus and driver, their food, tools and supplies. Without their passports they wouldn't be able to get back into California, let alone Canada. There were no phones at the farm and this was long before cell phones. Le asked Scott, "Can you take me back to the hotel?"

They got into the pick-up truck EV Free had rented for the construction and Le told Scott, "I'd like to have one of my youth leaders come with us." That volunteer's name was Steve Horrex who in more ways than one is a big guy. The three of them took off with Scott driving and Steve sandwiched in the middle. Little did Steve know, that life as he knew it—just like what happened to Scott—was about to be squeezed out of him.

Steve Horrex was born in New Westminster, Canada, near the Vancouver area of British Columbia and grew up with three older sisters in the Catholic Church. Mark Twain proclaimed, "Truth is stranger than fiction" and in Steve's case—growing up—it was. There were problems with Steve's mom and dad's marriage; his father ran off and married the babysitter, and Steve's mom married the milkman (no joke!). They would both remarry again later. Because of the divorce, the Horrex family was kicked out of the Catholic Church.

At the age of fifteen, when Steve's mom and her new husband decided to move seven hours north, Steve decided he had enough and moved out on his own. One of his sisters' signed for him on an apartment lease. He continued high school, worked in a retail lighting store and supported himself.

At seventeen, Steve finished high school, started working in construction and was invited to the EV Free Johnson Heights youth group. Steve was amazed to see teenagers his own age having such a good time. He couldn't figure that out. He had never experienced anything like it before, at least not without being high on something. That summer he joined the youth group on their Drewry Lake Fishing Trip. During the week, Pastor Spivey asked the great question, "Would you like Jesus Christ to come into your life? Are you willing to accept His forgiveness and accept Him as your Lord and Savior?" Steve thought about it and bartered, "OK God, you have a week. If you want me, you can change me in a week." Steve recalled, "While I was there, God changed my whole life forever. I decided not to do drugs, gave up old friends because that was part of the problem, and my life was changed forever."

When Steve returned home, he worked at changing his life and tried to give up swearing. He prayed to God and decided, if he didn't have anything nice to say, he wouldn't say anything at all. Consequently, for several weeks, Steve hardly spoke a word and became very quiet. He learned a lot about himself and started to grow and mature. He became involved with EV Free Johnson Heights which had a church body of about seven hundred people. Steve volunteered to help with their youth ministry and quickly was leading activities. After working in construction for two years, Steve realized almost everything he was doing for different contractors, he could do himself and he started his own construction company naming it "G & S Construction" standing for "God and Steve."

During that drive back to the hotel in San Diego, Steve asked Scott, "Why are you doing this?" Scott told Steve how God changed his life and how Amor started. Steve exclaimed, "Wow! I could never do something like that."

Then, in perfect unscripted unison, both Le and Scott chimed, "Never, say 'never' to God."

Steve was like, "Huh? What?"

Scott continued, "No, no. You don't want to be in that position. You say 'No' to God and just mark our words; it will be a challenge, because God will have His way with you one way or the other; the hard way or the easy way."

When they arrived back at the hotel, unbelievably, the brief case with all the cash and the group's passports was sitting on the hotel lobby floor, exactly where Le had left it; next to the chair he had been sitting in. It had been twelve hours since they left the busy hotel lobby and there it was, full of cash, just waiting for them.

When we lose or misplace something important, or when something seems to go terribly wrong, we typically ask, "Why God? Why is this happening to me?" or, "I can't believe this. What did I do to deserve this? What else can go wrong?" We usually think the worse. But truly, it is in times like this that God is at work. When a crisis occurs, changes take place in our lives that otherwise wouldn't happen. It's when things go wrong for all the right reasons. It was during that ride—back to the hotel and then back to the orphanage—where the wheels of Steve Horrex's twenty-one-year-old heart and brain were beginning to turn in a new and different direction.

When they arrived back at the orphanage, Scott wished them good luck and basically left them in the middle of the boonies.

The EV Free group's initial perception was to come down to Mexico and help poor people. Both EV Free and Amor had no experience in building an orphanage, which was good and bad. Everyone just knew they had to make it happen, and they did—start digging that is. It was heavy manual labor in the hot Mexican sun. They dug out the footing for the foundation, mixed and poured concrete, and constructed a four-foot wall of cement blocks around what would be the perimeter of the building. Steve fondly remembers, "It was a great week—it was everything—all of our lives were touched regardless of what we were doing."

What those EV Free volunteers returned home with filled a void in their lives. They were both surprised and joyful that *they* received so much out of the trip. For the first time, Steve saw reality; he could not "Out Give God." EV Free returned and continued to build the orphanage which took three years to complete and, incredibly, out of that first group of thirty-six volunteers, eight went into full-time ministry because of their Amor experience!

Before Steve went down, he thought he was doing so much by being involved with his church and their youth group. He thought he was doing everything he needed to be a good Christian, and for somebody looking at Steve's life from the outside in, they would agree. But Steve, now knew God had a bigger plan for him and he was overwhelmed with the feeling of: "I'm not doing enough."

Steve struggled, and a friend reminded him of Proverbs 3:5-6, "Trust in the Lord with all your heart, lean not upon your own understanding, and in all your ways acknowledge Him and He will guide and direct your path."

Steve asked himself, "What are the desires of my heart?" His answer, "I love construction. I love working with my hands and creating, and I love the aspect of working and seeing smiling kids."

Six months after the Canadians returned home, Scott received a phone call. "Hey, remember that guy named Steve who took the ride with you back to San Diego when you said, 'never say never to God?' Remember that kid?"

Scott remembered, "Oh yeah, Steve, how you doing?"

Steve answered, "You were right."

This time it was Scott who said, "Huh?"

Steve continued, "You were right about never say never to God because I can't stop thinking about it. I can't stop thinking about what I saw. I can't stop thinking about what you said. I can't stop thinking about God. Hey, I've already talked to my church and I told them that

God wants me to go to Mexico and work with you guys. I've already told them! The church is behind me. They want to send me."

Scott pointed out, "We don't have any money to hire you." Little did Steve know, Scott and Gayla had been praying for God to provide someone who knew construction and would finance their own position.

Steve said, "That doesn't matter, I'll live on whatever it takes. The church is willing to help support me and I'm ready to sell everything."

As soon as the decision was made, Steve knew it was the right one. He packed his truck with just his clothes and tools. Everything else he sold or gave away.

Scott thought what Steve was doing was bigger than what he had done, because when he did it, he didn't own a lot of things or have a business of his own. Steve started and built his construction company from the ground up. He had employees, a house, cars and lots of stuff. Steve Horrex acted on faith and a calling. He got rid of everything and moved in with Gayla and Scott, who six months earlier had become Mr. and Mrs. Congdon.

Amor Ministries started in 1980. Steve Horrex joined Scott and Gayla in 1982 and both Scott and Gayla consider Steve to be one of the founders. When Steve, Gayla and Scott started working together, they would confide in each other and laugh that they had no idea what they were doing but agreed, "So what, let's just keep doing it."

Scott noted having Steve as a Canadian was an asset because Mexicans love Canadians. Canadians don't carry any of the pretentious baggage, arrogance and difficult history with Mexico like the U.S. does. With a Canadian, Mexicans are like, "Oh, a Canadian, we love Canadians!" Steve's Canadian presence with Amor Ministries helped open doors that otherwise would have been closed.

Chapter Six

The Tijuana Dump

"We're building homes because of our love for God."
Amor Ministries

Scott made Tijuana Dump runs with garbage from the orphanage and he'd often return with a child in desperate condition. Scott's trash runs were a two-way operation; bring the orphanage garbage to the dump and return with society's garbage—an orphan child. When Scott first started working at the orphanage there were fifty kids and in short order, because of his garbage runs there were seventy-five. The Orphanage Director told Scott, "You've got to either stop going to the dump or you've got to stop bringing kids back."

When recalling the Tijuana Dump, Scott remembers, "The orphanage was bad but the dump was devastating. I mean piles of garbage everywhere and fires. The children were just covered in dirt, no haircuts and most of them just had on a pair of shorts. They looked like ancient cave kids. Just packs of them, flies everywhere. There were families scraping out an existence and there were families of just kids, street kids. They were homeless. It was a mixture of everything. The kids all hung together. You couldn't tell which one was a pure orphan or which one had a Mom or a Grandma somewhere, most of the times the father was absent. The stench was horrible. I was shocked. Words can't describe the devastation. That was the deepest devastation that I have ever experienced in the ministry—seeing the Tijuana Dump and seeing what they lived in; stacks of shipping pallets or just tarps and stuff with garbage all around them. They'd carve out a hole in the garbage and just put a tarp over the top of it. Yet, the neatest kids but sort of glassy eyed; they were very sick. They'd eat the food out of the garbage. That's how they'd subsist and, so they weren't healthy. When the Orphanage Director said you can't bring the kids back to the orphanage anymore I was like, 'We can't not do that.'"

When Steve came on board with Amor he worked at the Tecate orphanage until it was completed in 1984. When Amor finished the orphanage, Steve, Scott and Gayla got to thinking about how it took almost three years to construct an orphanage for twenty-five kids, and the Tijuana Dump had more than 250 kids. At that rate, it would take their entire lifetime to try and build enough orphanages for these kids.

Steve joined Scott on his garbage runs, and during Steve's first trip he visited a little church. When he looked around, he saw walls coming apart and the roof was leaking. Steve offered to help and for a time did a hodgepodge of repairs. He told Scott and Gayla they could do more and suggested, "The first thing we do is just start making their little shelter a little better."

Scott liked the idea and thought, "If we can't take the kids to the orphanage, maybe we can do something for them right there." Steve suggested he could design a simple structure. However, one of the many problems associated with the people living at the dump is they were squatters and didn't own the property.

Steve designed an eleven foot by twenty-two-foot house with four by four-inch corner posts dug into the garbage, two feet into the ground. Framing went up between the posts and wood siding was screwed in. They used eight and twelve-foot length 2 X 4 framing, eight feet on one side, sloping to seven feet on the other, creating a sloped roof. The post holes were cemented in such a way they could be broken out, with the whole house capable of being taken apart, put on top of a car, driven down the street and rebuilt. Amor started building these uniquely designed homes and larger groups from throughout the United States and Canada volunteered to come down and build Amor houses.

Diet and food was a problem for those living in the garbage where people scavenged and ate the bacteria infested trash. Inhabitants were suffering from all kinds of disease, parasites and gastrointestinal disorders. Amor recognized the problem, worked with the city officials and were successful in getting them subsidized tortillas—the Mexican food staple.

Amor built over three hundred homes for more than a thousand people from mid-1985 until 1987 and literally transformed the Tijuana Dump. They also built a school, a store, a medical clinic, a playground and a church. Amor built a housing development right on top of the city's garbage pit and once people started living in those homes a vibrant community developed. Miraculously, today, that city garbage pile is gone because the community rose up and protested, "This is no longer a dump, this is our community and the government shouldn't be allowed to dump garbage here anymore because people live here, there are children here, we have a school and a church here." After many meetings and outcries from the community, Amor Ministries and the local pastors, the government gave in and moved the Tijuana Dump! They moved it out of the area and didn't allow any new squatters to move in.

What Amor built was called "The City of Love" and "The "Easter Egg City" because of all the brilliant Mexican colors families painted their Amor homes with; greens and oranges, turquoise and purples, reds and yellows. It was an amazing transformation. Before, when you went to the dump, it was hideous, and now after three years it looked like an Easter Egg Basket with colors everywhere.

Amor never proselytized about what they were doing. They just did it. Whenever anyone asked, they answered, "We're building homes for the love of God." Many eyes and hearts were opened. Individuals' perception of self-worth changed by having a roof over their heads and a place they could call home.

Issues regarding faith changed, whereas before, most of the inhabitants didn't believe in God, or thought, "If there is a God, how could he allow us to live like this?" Now they were eating better, they went to church, got a good night's sleep and when they went looking for a job, they held their heads up. And many of them found work, whereas before, nobody would take a second look at them.

Steve got to know the community officials and asked them, "Why can't you give these people title to their homes? That way they could own them, nobody could take it away from them; they would have a sense of permanence and security for their family." Amor worked on this and in time, every home given to a family would include their name on the title to the property. It became one of the most important requirements in Amor's ministry: Amor would build the home, provided the family received a vested interest in the title to the property. The community was also asked by the city government what did they want to call their community, and they responded with "Community Independence."

When Gayla looked back at the transformation of the Tijuana Dump she recalled, "I don't think I realized until Steve came up with the idea of building houses at the Tijuana Dump how much a home is tied to a person's self-esteem; the ability to provide for a roof over a family's head. I remember a situation where the Mexican pastors came to us and said there was a crisis where the dad was just a nightmare, the family had five kids and the dad decided he can't do this anymore. He said, 'I don't have a job. I don't know how to get a job. I can't get a job. I can't provide. It's a terrible life. Let's find an orphanage to put the kids in. You go live with your family. I'll go find a job in the United States and I'll send money and hopefully we can work our way back to each other.' They wanted us to build a home for this family and we did. People are transformed by having a home. When you have a home, you have a place to call your own and you see the world differently and all of a sudden you have hope, there's light at the end of the tunnel. It is something that connects everything back together. Consequentially, the dad felt he could get a job, and he did. He got a job and that family stayed together."

People ask Amor all the time about immigration saying, "You're doing your part to keep people in Mexico."

Amor's response: "No, we're doing our job to keep families together."

Gayla explains, "People don't understand about the Mexicans, because they love their country. I don't know what percentage of Mexicans would go some place to live like the United States if they didn't have to. But I don't think it would be very high. We don't properly understand. They passionately love their country. And they just want to stay together, and they don't know where to turn. You and I both would do whatever it took to provide for our family and they're no different, they want the same things for their families that we do. One of their options when they don't have enough money to provide for their family is to go to the United States to find work. But I have seen families transformed by having a house, something which we take for granted. You provide a home, it is a big self-worth issue and it helps a man find work. When I lived at that orphanage, I realized that every one of those children had a roof over their head, had three square meals a day, had school and they were loved. But for the most part, every one of them would rather be back together with their family. Of course, there were some who shouldn't have gone back to whatever environment they came from for good reasons. But every kid who was put in that orphanage for economic reasons would rather have lived in poverty with their family."

The Tijuana Dump had two sections; a lower area and an upper area. Most squatters eventually migrated to the upper area. There was one woman who was thought to have gone crazy when a fire had started in her home and both of her children were killed. Neither the lower or upper areas would have anything to do with her. She was the outcast of the outcast; a pariah. She lived on top of the trash in a teepee held up with 2 X 4 posts and a ragged carpet tossed over it. Steve knew she was mentally ill. Every time he'd drive to the upper dump to check on the Amor construction, he'd stop and check in on her. He'd ask her how she was doing; did she need anything, and he'd give her part of his lunch.

One day, while Steve was driving down the hill, she flagged him down. Steve thought she needed help with something. When he stopped, Steve realized, she was inviting him to lunch. Steve knew the food was coming from the garbage and he'd be eating trash. He knew he'd probably get sick from whatever he ate. But the woman had prepared something for him and it was her way of saying "Thank You." To her, it was everything and Steve knew he couldn't say no. He knew God wanted him to get alongside this crazy woman, be with her and eat lunch with her. Steve admitted, "This was a risk I was willing to take. I had my Pepto-Bismol stuck in the door panel for when I wasn't feeling well, and I thought I would survive one way or the other. I sat down in the trash and had a taco with her and I knew the impact it had on her; it was huge. I knew it was her way of saying thank you but in the same way, it had a huge impact on me because I knew that's exactly where I needed to be. Of course, consequently, I was sick for over three months afterwards. I went to the doctors and was told I had some type of bug, that it was going to take time to get rid of and I had to eat dry toast, Jell-O and water for three months."

It was miraculous how the changes and transformations just kept on coming. When Amor first started building homes, the people living at the dump didn't know how long Amor was going to be there and some were getting into fights over who was going to get a home. Two sisters beat each other up. Amor called a meeting and warned them, "God doesn't want to have anything to do with this if you're going to fight. God will provide for all of you. It will take some time but you will all get a home. But if you're going to disrespect God and you're going to fight amongst yourselves, we're going to leave." People realized what was at stake and some started to cry, they apologized to Scott, Steve and Gayla, started thanking them and pleaded with them to stay.

One of the best testimonies came from a very old woman, "You know, before you came we had no hope. We were going to live in the dump and we were going to die in the dump. Nothing was ever going to change for us, and we just figured God didn't care. I now have a house! I never thought I'd ever have a house. I never thought in my life I'd have a house. I have a home! I have hope now, and I go to church now, and I know God has a plan for my life." And then she added, "I can dream now. Why I'm dreaming that... that I'll get a Cadillac someday!"

There was a pause. Steve and Scott looked at each other and asked, "Oh no, what have we done?"

Then she explained, "No, no, no, I'm just joking" and everyone laughed. She went on and acknowledged, "You see, we could never have even joked about that before; the thought that any of us could have a car. We can now dream that someday some of us will even have a car."

Today, it is no joke, because those original Amor homes are unrecognizable. They've been added on to with second stories and some have grown three to four times their original size. They have gardens and fences around them, there are garages and cars everywhere, even Cadillacs.

Amor learned from the beginning to work through local Mexican churches. They learned it was the local churches and people living in the communities that knew better than anyone who were in the greatest need. Amor learned if they relied on their own observations and opinions, they'd be making mistakes all the time. Through Amor's eyes, it appeared everyone was in need but clearly, there were people in greater need than others.

Amor understood when they built a home for one family they needed to be cognizant of how the neighbors felt. It was an issue. Amor realized to be effective, it was important to take the decision-making process regarding who received the homes out of their hands. They understood it was important to have the pastors who lived in those communities let Amor know who was "the poorest of the poor" and who should get an Amor home.

The only way Amor could know what that looked like was through the eyes of the local pastors and community members who knew the families, their history and needs. Amor wasn't in Mexico to create a name for Amor, they wanted to support what God was doing in Mexico and consequentially became an outreach ministry supporting the local churches.

After Amor had built a home for everyone living at the dump they asked the local pastors, "What more can we do to help? Do you have other areas? Do you have other families?"

The answer of course was "Yes, there are many other families in need." Just like Tubby, Amor would begin again, and for the next thirty plus years has brought groups from all over the world to Mexico to build Amor houses.

Most orphans in Mexico are not true orphans, 80-90% of those kids have parents or at the very least a grandparent. Gayla lived at TCM for a year, she knew where those kids came from, who their families were, and she knew those kids wanted to be at home with their families. They didn't care if their home was a garbage pit. For Amor, when they first started building houses it was because they couldn't build enough orphanages fast enough. Often, they were told, it would be better to build a church or a school, and often they did build churches, schools and medical clinics in communities. But it became Amor's number one goal to help keep families together by building homes.

Scott explains it's the reason why there are no orphanages in the United States. They've been replaced by foster care programs, and as difficult as that is, it's better than an orphanage. In an orphanage it's difficult to teach children how to parent, how they would someday need to take care of their own children. Orphans don't learn how to parent and raise a family, they learn how to be an orphan. They don't know what it's like to be a husband or a wife and when they have kids, they send them to an orphanage, just like what happened to them. Amor breaks that cycle by keeping families together, by giving them a home where the family can stay together and grow together. Moms can be Mom, dads can be Dad, brothers and sisters can live together.

Mexico is a Third World country where poverty, corruption, crime, disease, unemployment, starvation, homelessness, and broken homes are prevalent. When Scott thinks in terms of poverty, he thinks in terms of losing babies. Those are the families and situations that impact him the most, when he feels the physical and mental effects of poverty.

Extreme poverty is when a mother who receives no assistance or medical aid lives in a shack and is caring for her child who is brain damaged and can't speak. Amor learns about situations where the father is blind and cannot work, the baby just died, or there is a paralyzed child inside a shack. Amor builds homes for those devastated families, and those are the families the church loves to love. When Amor builds homes for families who are in desperate need, the mother and the blind father thank God with tears of joy for having sent them angels.

Scott, Gayla, and Steve, along with the Amor staff all agree that giving a family a home is the most amazing experience, and they have done it thousands of times. Scott says it's surreal knowing they're changing families in such a profound way. It's an incredible last day when the group that built the house, holds hands, prays together with the family and gives them the keys to their new home. It is a transforming moment to give a family a home you just built, knowing it will change their lives.

Mexico is a macho culture. Prideful barriers are shattered when a home is given to a family, when tears run down the faces of men and boys who never thought they'd have a home, realizing, with an Amor home, they have hope for their family to stay together.

Equally amazing and transforming is what happens to the groups of Americans, Canadians, Australians, Europeans and Africans who could have been at home or on vacation doing a hundred other things but instead chose to come to Mexico, take a week of their time, camp out, pay for all the building materials, and build an Amor home. The entire process, from beginning to end, results in Godly relationships being built when these groups share their time and their money. They live, work, travel, play, and pray together (some for the first time). They get to know each other as well as interact with the Mexican families, and in many instances, have life-changing experiences. They're not just a construction company or a government crew that came, built, and left. These people shared an incredible time of their life together and the Mexican families will never forget them.

When Steve looks back after thirty-five years he says, "Every group goes down with a different perspective, but God seems to work with each one of those situations and scenarios and lives are changed at both ends of it, not only for the people you are serving but also for the people that serve!"

Hebrews 3:3-4, "Jesus has been found worthy of greater honor than Moses, just as the builder of a house has greater honor than the house itself. For every house is built by someone but God is the builder of everything." The house versus the builder and the builder of the house has greater honor than the house itself? Everyone who builds Amor homes sees how those homes will transform the lives of those who will live in it. It seems that the house *is* greater than the builder. Scott explains, "The tangible thing is building houses but that's really not what it's about—it's about changing lives, which is so very hard to explain to people; 'Come down and change lives! Come down and have your life changed!' Building homes is one of the most tangible, physical needs these families have, and some groups get so caught up in building the house, Amor has to tell them, 'You don't have to finish the house during your first week, it will get done.' What really is even more important is what is happening in your life on that trip, what is happening to the life of that Mexican family, and if you have built a house but you haven't built a relationship, what's the point?"

The families Amor builds homes for have lived on the streets or in shacks with dirt floors made of discarded wood, corrugated metal, tires, pieces of tarp, and cardboard. They use old newspapers for wallpaper. Families with one, two, three, even four and five children, scrape out a living on as little as $240 per month. That's $60 per week. Most receive no medical benefits and don't go to the doctor until they're dying, and then it's too late. Many children don't attend school because to go to school in Mexico they must have a uniform and school supplies costing $35 plus per child. The water they drink, cook, and wash with is often unfiltered and contaminated when they receive it from private delivery trucks that pump into open storage barrels sitting in the hot sun or a little piece of shade all day long. There is little to no electricity, and toilets are just holes in the ground.

It is difficult for anyone who has a home of their own or comes from a family with any wherewithal to understand what it is like to be poor… dirt poor. Most of us will readily admit how horrible it must be to be poor, but the truth is, we can only grasp at it intellectually. Then, all so often, we quickly dismiss it while we focus on our needs; our family, our friends and the world in which we live. The poor live minute-by-minute, hour by hour, trying to scratch out an existence with little to no hope, not even dreaming, just subsisting. They die in need while many others die in greed.

It is all too true and unfortunate that so very often, people who are in positions to help develop misguided opinions and attitudes towards the poor. It is a deplorable state of affairs when individuals and groups elevate their sense of self-worth at the expense of others. Mankind has often found a convenient way to look down on their fellow man, to look down on different groups and individuals of different socio-economic stature, class, race, religion, and culture.

Family is everything, especially when you have nothing and are dirt poor. The joy for those families is their children, who in their youth and innocence have a happiness about them that must be seen and experienced to be believed. It is infectious. What those kids know is they've got Mom and hopefully Dad's love, brothers, sisters, aunts, uncles, cousins, and grandparents who also love them, even though they go to bed hungry most all the time. As in any child, they possess a creative spirit and figure out how to play with dirt, rocks, and discarded cardboard.

Scott remembers seeing a group of little boys in a circle at the orphanage, heads hovering and butted together. Scott asked, "What are you guys doing?" They backed up, so he could see. In the middle were four boys, one was carefully holding down a bumble bee's leg with one finger, another was holding down the other leg, another was holding down the wing, while another was carefully tying a thread around the bee's body. When he was done, they all backed away, a boy tapped the bee and it took off flying, and those little boys went around the room taking turns flying the bee on the string.

Children will be children—even in the poorest of conditions, they'll figure out how to play with something within their environment. They don't need a PlayStation, a cell phone, a computer, an iPod, Nintendo, or even TV. However, as the years go by, children living in poverty quickly lose their innocence, hopes, and dreams. They get involved in violence, drugs, robbery, and prostitution. One of the most horrible realities of being poor occurs when a family has little to nothing to eat. Parents will ask themselves, "What am I willing to do? How far am I willing to go to feed and clothe my children?"

Their life gets backed into a corner and somebody offers them money to smuggle drugs; money equaling months of wages—that's if they could find a job. That illegal offer becomes the only hope they have to put food on the table, that unethical opportunity coming from evil preying upon the weak. Gayla says, "Being poor means you are dealing with a situation where you don't have a place to turn. If you are poor, your family is probably poor, so you can't go to your dad and get money. You just don't have the resources. There's no place to turn. And you have to be honest, there is corruption in Mexico. When a person enters that life of corruption and drugs, they live in fear and there's no turning back. Going up against someone, against a gang, is it worth it? It might cost you your life, which might even be OK but if it costs the life of your child…"

The Amor experience brings people together, people from different worlds. Amor passionately believes in getting people out of their comfort zones. To build an Amor home, people get alongside each other, work together and through that process, away from their home and everyday securities. Many realize, we are all made in God's image, an image of trust and goodness.

Scott, Steve, and Gayla hear stories every year from volunteers who started going on Amor trips decades ago. Volunteers tell them, a young man saw them, remembered them, walked up to them and calls out, "Hey, I'm Raphael, remember me!" They remember you—they will never forget you. They invite you into their home to say hello to their family and eat a meal with them. You are an instant celebrity and you feel at home in the most welcomed sense.

One of the most powerful moments for Amor groups is the campfire or tented evening worship. Students and adults are busy working together during the day, but they're also like sponges, seeing life and poverty like they'd never seen before. It's hard to process when you're on a worksite hammering, mixing cement, and cutting wood, plus it's often hot—you're tired and sweating. You're working hard but you're also playing with those beautiful Mexican kids.

When you get back to the campfire or community tent, after you've eaten a well-deserved meal, it's a little cooler, the stars are out, your body is bone tired but you're thinking, "Why am I here? Why does God have me here?" and "Why does God allow this poverty, this place?" Your group starts talking about the experience, about life and often somebody reads the Gospel with many hearing it for the first time. Both adults and kids say, "This trip has changed my life. This trip has opened my eyes to things I never imagined. This has made me wonder, ask what life is all about. How can I be living the life I live?"

The trip becomes a time of deep personal introspection, and amazing conversations and discussions take place about what's important, about helping others. It's one of the most powerful moments in the church and people's lives, and it's not just talk, it's about taking action. Scott says sitting at a campfire in Mexico, under the stars, talking and asking, "Why me... why God? That is church at its best."

Amor started as a grassroots organization and has remained faithful and loyal to their roots, continuing with the same principles of integrity that have guided them through the past. Amor is supported by more than 1,000 groups and churches, along with individuals throughout the United States, Canada, Australia, New Zealand, Ireland, Scotland, Wales, England, Central America, South Korea and of all places, Africa.

Scott says, "It's just like what Toc H and Project Mexico did for me—we need to bring people together. So often we live our lives with blinders on, caught up with ourselves, the perception of the world we live in, opinionated and biased towards others, when the truth is, we don't even have a clue."

By the late 1980s Mike Yaconelli was a nationally sought-after speaker and was receiving national recognition for the books he'd written along with his achievement with YS and their conventions. Mike started bringing groups down from Northern California and became a national ambassador for Amor Ministries. Mike was so moved by his Amor experiences, he asked, "You come down, give one week of your life and change the life of a Mexican family forever. What would happen if you gave your whole life?"

Scott says his greatest joys in the ministry are present every day. He refers back to one of his most touching moments, when Amor had just finished building a house for a mother and her five-year-old son who had been living in a horrible shack. Reflecting, Scott explains, "It's what I think about when I have hard days." Scott said after the youth group left, the mother walked up to him with her five-year-old son, tears running down her cheeks and cried, "I have nothing to give you but this picture. Thank you! Thank you for building my home."

Scott looked at the picture and realized, "Oh, that's him, your son."

The woman put her arm around her son and said, "No, that's not him but you saved his life."

Scott questioned, "This isn't him?"

She replied, "No" and explained how four months earlier in December, when the cold rains came, she was living in a small shack with a dirt floor, a cardboard bed and used plastic bags to try to keep herself, her son, and six-month-old baby girl dry. The wind howled through all the openings and the rain kept coming in, soaking everything, including them. She held her children, trying to keep them warm but it was impossible. Her baby started shaking and trembled throughout the night. By morning her baby was gasping for air. The mother was able to get a neighbor to find someone with a car willing to take them to the hospital where the baby died of pneumonia. The picture she gave Scott was the only thing she had to give, and it was of her tiny baby girl. The woman said, "You may not have been able to save my daughter but you've saved my son's life." Her last words to Scott were, "Never! Never stop building homes."

Scott has kept that picture in his wallet and often, whenever he has a bad day asks himself, "Why am I doing this?" He pulls out the picture, looks at it, and says, "Thank you Lord."

Gayla has never been one to get together and just talk about things, she's always taking care of the immediate needs at hand, looking forward and planning for Amor's tomorrows.

After twenty-five years in the ministry, Gayla found herself in a quandary. When her mother Virginia developed the early stages of Alzheimer's, Gayla brought her mom home to live with her family. On New Year's Eve 1999, as the world was entering the 21st Century and everyone feared the threatened disaster of Y2K, Virginia died, and the contrived Y2K fear—like many of our fears—evaporated into nothing. Afterwards, Scott and Gayla's son, Jordan, left home and went away to college on a football scholarship. Gayla found herself emotionally and physically exhausted. She took some needed time off and was thinking about retiring from the ministry. After a while, Scott asked his wife and partner, "Well, are you going to come back to the ministry full-time, part-time? What do you want to do? I kind of need you to decide so we can make plans."

Gayla answered, "I want to make sure I'm doing what God wants me to do."

Scott asked her to return to Mexico with him during Amor's 25th anniversary. During that trip, God spoke to Gayla through her interaction with two grandmothers for whom Amor had just built their 10,000th home. They were sisters, one was eighty-five years old and the other seventy-five and neither had ever had a home of their own before. They had lived their entire lives on the streets or in a shack. They told Gayla, "We'd never thought we'd ever have a home of our own."

Gayla was so moved by the joy of those grandmothers finally getting a home she realized, "Now I know what the next part of my life is supposed to be," and she returned to Amor Ministry full-time saying, "I am as passionate about what we do today, as I was when I was twenty-two years old, when I first went to Mexico."

Amor volunteers have gone on to become doctors, lawyers, nurses, teachers, community leaders, missionaries, pastors, businessmen, and businesswomen. Some of them bring new churches and groups down to Mexico because of their past Amor experiences. Counting all the volunteers, the members of churches that support them, the Mexican families, Amor staff, and interns, literally millions of lives have been impacted. Lives have been transformed and in many ways, Amor has helped change the world for the better.

Scott learned he can talk and talk about it, but there's nothing like getting volunteers down to Mexico. Scott looks back in amazement, "Now, I can't believe God has us bringing thousands of people to Mexico for a week at a time and then letting us watch what He does with them." Scott tells groups the same thing the Orphanage Director told him, "God has you here for a reason, just like he did me. You just have to be open to what God is doing."

Scott and Gayla cannot go anywhere in the world and not bump into somebody who hasn't been involved with or heard of Amor Ministries. When they began they understood, "This is God's mission. There's poverty starring us in the face. We've got to eliminate it. We've got to do what we can right here, right now." Along the way they learned the beauty of building homes, keeping children out of orphanages, and helping families stay together. They learned to support the local community and to work as an outreach through pastors and churches. They learned that those who receive a home must also receive the title to the property. They learned how to locate the poor and build homes for them, and along the way have witnessed the most amazing blessing—just get people out of their comfort zones and God will do the rest—God will perform miracles.

Epilogue

Scott Congdon
Founder/CEO Amor Ministries

I remember the day Dan Irving called me and said I didn't know him, but he had a story to tell that could change the understanding of my life. It was the curiosity that got my attention. So, I agreed to have a meeting with him.

From the trenches of World War I to the trenches of a Mexican dump, seven decades later. Who would have imagined? From along the Western Front and a war described as the Great War and The War to End All Wars, to the battle lines to end poverty in families and children living among burning trash and caustic smoke.

Dan described how great men fought in the first world war long before my time and had served their countries in horrific conditions and agony. I was told – incredibly – how these brave men and women laid the groundwork for the path of my life, my family and Amor Ministries. It was as if I was seeing the tapestry found in an old attic with traces of our ancestry, the people who went before us, the people who served and sacrificed, the people whose shoulders we were now standing upon. These were the servant hearted who God used to form this tapestry in my life, long before I had any hint of God's plans.

Why God chose an unlikely group like the team at Amor, only God knows. Why He took two young, inexperienced, idealistic kids like Gayla and me to the trenches of a Mexican dump, only He knows. What we do know is, if God calls, and we ignore it, or don't listen, we may very well miss the greatest opportunity of our lives. Perhaps, it took someone like Tubby Clayton, the "Impudent Dreamer" to cast aside caution, sensibilities, and fear to climb head on into the most tragic and ghastly conditions man has managed to perpetuate upon his fellow man.

As young people seeking a path to show God's love for the poor in Mexico—though we knew nothing about Tubby Clayton, Toc H, Dan

Irving, Wayne Kistner or Coleman Jennings (C.J.)—it most certainly
was not experience, training or knowhow that lead us. No, it surely
wasn't us. It was God who led us to create a Christian ministry to
house and feed the poor and connect this ministry throughout the
world.

Amor Ministries completed building homes for every family and
orphan in the Tijuana Dump in 1988. After building 600+ homes in the
Dump and working with fifty plus youth and adult groups from the
West Coast, Amor had reached a junction. Where to now? The answer
was right in front of us. As we built those homes, we were involved
with the community and local pastors. Those local pastors all along
were saying, "Please, come build more homes in Tijuana." Throughout
Tijuana, many Mexicans were living in abject poverty, on dirt floors,
in shacks made of cardboard, shipping pallets, used lumber, plastic and
rocks; anything they could find. They were living in open fields,
canyons and on hillsides in small settlements. Our next mission, which
continues to this day, had already been determined and we expanded
by building homes in Tijuana.

Word of what Amor Ministries was continuing to do spread. Pastors
came to us asking Amor to build in their communities. We again
expanded by building homes in Tecate, Rosarito, Mexicali, Puerto
Penasco, Juarez and the Yucatan Peninsula and on the Apache
Reservations, in San Carlos, Arizona. Not only were we building
homes, we were being asked to fill other needs. Amor constructed
schools, stores, churches, community centers, police stations, fire
stations and medical clinics. Not only did we expand our construction
projects, we expanded our volunteer base worldwide with youth and
adult groups from the United States, Canada, Australia, the United
Kingdom, South Africa and Mexico. We have developed programs
and ministries that provide water filtration systems, school supplies,
backpacks, bibles, eye glasses, blankets, food banks and job
opportunities. During peak construction periods, Amor was attracting
25,000 volunteers a year from around the world and building up to
1,100 homes a year. One of the most amazing blessings was that all
the volunteers and groups paid for their transportation, food, lodging
and most of the construction costs.

In 2007 Amor Ministries started building homes in South Africa
and is now building homes in one of the poorest communities in the

world, Soweto. Building homes here presented many challenges. Yet, those challenges were no different from when Amor first started. We were new to building homes in South Africa and our learning curve was in front of us. In South Africa, they do not build with wood like we do in Mexico and there were post-apartheid politics at play. There was no money for the construction, but the need for housing was so great. Amor went forward on a wing and a prayer. Miraculously, everything fell into place. Today, Amor South Africa builds homes with international volunteer groups and educates South African locals how to construct Amor houses. One of the amazing ministries created by Gayla is Women of Strength, where women from around the world meet in South Africa, build homes and in the process, build each other up.

A core value of Amor Ministries is to serve directly along families and those in need while working in partnership with local churches. In my wife's book, *Disrupted*, she wrote: "Jordan (our son) told us about two dads who approached him during the house build, begging to work with the group in return for food for their respective families. Jordan had felt helpless when confronted by the need and humility that had driven those men to beg. The feelings grew into guilt because he had grown up with everything he needed. He struggled to understand why, and he just couldn't eat." This impacted Jordan profoundly and he has since dedicated his life along with his wife, April to serving others fulltime through Amor Ministries.

Making a difference through the joyful privilege of serving others is something Amor celebrates by bringing people together to provide life changing, transformational experiences that manifest the justice, kindness and humility of Jesus Christ. Not only are the lives of the families and those in need transformed, the lives of volunteers and those who come to serve are forever changed. It constantly amazes me to hear how a volunteer's life was impacted by their Amor experience, and to learn what they are now doing to help change this world for the better.

I feel abundantly blessed to now know this integral piece of our history, and I feel so connected to this story. Not only are we connected to the past in Heart of the Poppy, this history is linked to everyday presence and future; transcending time, people, relationships and geography.

The future of Amor is one of responding to the needs of poverty and homelessness. We have learned to trust in God and move forward. While money and infrastructure always remain a challenge, hope is an amazing thing, and when applied to faith, all things are possible. At Amor, we recognize the importance of serving and helping others, understanding they can be our neighbors down the street, across the border or around the globe. May we not pass them by but always live the life of a Good Samaritan. Our mission continues to be based on actions which relies upon our faith in God through Jesus Christ. Keeping families together by providing homes, clean water and training are key, while continuing to work through local churches, pastors, youth and adult groups.

I hope this story inspires and moves you to celebrate your ability to serve. When you come across those in need, what can you do? What are you willing to do? If you move forward and work with a ministry such as Amor, you will no doubt be blessed.

I would love for you to join us in this continuing story and in furthering this Godly adventure. In that effort, you can phone me directly at 512-270-4207, internationally at +1(512) 270-4207 or you can phone Amor Ministries at 619-662-1200.

Toc H

Toc H in the UK is a membership organization managed by a board of trustees and governed by Royal Charter first granted in 1922. It is a registered charity. Toc H stands proud in its mission to bring people together in reconciliation while reaching out to those members of society most in need.

Toc H members seek to ease the burdens of others through acts of service. Historically, the Toc H movement has been responsible for starting or collaborating in some of the most innovative forms of social service.

Toc H is also active through its partners. Over the years, many projects that began in Toc H now exist as independent organizations including the Winant-Clayton Volunteers; the School Under the Sky, the Associated Friends of Khasdobir and Amor Ministries.

As mentioned above, Fellowship sits alongside Service as a fundamental aim of Toc H and many branches still meet regularly to share in this aspect. Toc H is a Christian based Movement that welcomes those of other, and of no religion, into its fold and chooses to promote Christianity through deed and example rather than by preaching. There is some ceremony involved in branch meetings most notably the act of taking Light. There are some overseas pockets of Toc H – particularly in Australia and Belgium – which carry out activities in the name of Toc H. In post-colonial countries such as Zimbabwe, remaining members make vital contributions to the community. Toc H also continues to maintain strong ties with Talbot House in Belgium.

Toc H branches and members continue in the UK; Australia; India; Zimbabwe, South Africa; Gibraltar; France; California and elsewhere. The commonality of this worldwide movement is its shared ethos which is best summed up in the Four Points of the Compass which expressed the fundamental beliefs of Toc H and were originally drawn up in 1920. These are Fellowship (To Love Widely); Service (To Build Bravely); Fairmindedness (To Think Fairly); and the Kingdom of God (To Witness Humbly).

<u>Toc H Head Office</u>
P.O. Box 15824
Birmingham
B13 3JU
International Phone: +44-121-443-3552
U.K. Phone: 0121 44 33 55 2
Email: *info@toch.org.uk*
Patron: Members of the Royal Family &
Her Majesty The Queen

Amor Ministries

Headquartered in San Diego, California, Amor Ministries is committed to providing groups, families and individuals with life-changing, Christ-centered mission trip opportunities. When Amor began in 1980 the poorest families sent their children away to orphanages in Mexico because they could not provide for them. Rather than being full of children without parents, orphanages cared for kids whose parents loved them so much they were sent away to provide for their general needs.

After learning this, Amor's founders decided to do something about it. Throughout our history, our main purpose has been to provide adequate housing for needy families in order to keep families together! Amor's work began in Tijuana, Mexico, and the ministry has expanded to Puerto Penasco and Ciudad Juarez, Mexico; Delmas, South Africa; the San Carlos Apache Reservation in Globe, Arizona; Australia; and Amor Europe based in the U.K.

Amor works with local pastors in each ministry location to help ensure the ministry is meeting the greatest needs of the community.

More than 375,000 participants and volunteers have worked with Amor building 20,000+ homes for the poor and 357 churches planted or built.

Amor programs included:

Family Camp: An all-inclusive trip for families of all sizes and ages. They meet in San Diego and Amor coordinates the trip from there. Families build houses for the poor along other families; working together. Each day includes worship, interaction with the local community and a theme party.

Global Gathering: An all-inclusive trip for individuals, families or groups as large as fifty. It takes place in Cancun, Mexico every two years and includes world renowned speakers and participants from all over the world, while participating in building a home alongside a family in need. A life changing experience that promotes how you can live justice for the rest of your life.

Women of Strength: An all-inclusive trip for women ages ten and up. Join women from around the world in a week of house building, connecting relationships, and a down-right good time. Trips are being offered in Tijuana and South Africa. A personal and cultural experience.

Amor Three Day: An all-inclusive trip for individuals and groups of less than fifteen people. Open to all ages (under eighteen must be with a guardian). Just sign up and come. Bring your clothes, your sleeping bag and your passport to San Diego and Amor Ministries will take care of the rest.

For more information, write to 3636 Camino Del Rio North, Suite 215, San Diego CA 92108, visit *www.amor.org,* or call 619-662-1200.

Bibliography & Resources

Chapter 1: The Western Front

Agtmaal, van, Frederik. *I Have a Rendezvous with Death at Some Disputed Barricade - Poetry of the First World War* (Equilibriums, Belgium - 2002)

Joseph, M., Alvin, Jr.& Editors of American Heritage *The American Heritage History of World War I* (American Heritage Publishing - 1964)

Bull, Stephen. *World War I Trench Warfare* (Osprey Publishing - 2002)

Chapman, Paul. *Cameos of the Western Front - A Haven in Hell, Ypres Sector 1914-1918* (Leo Cooper/an imprint of Pen & Sword Books Limited, South Yorkshire - 2000)

Everett, Susanne. *World War I - An Illustrated History* (Exeter Books, New York - 1984)

Guttman, Jon. *SPA124 Lafayette Escadrille - American Volunteer Airmen in World War I* (Osprey Publishing - 2004)

Hitler, Adolf. *Mein Kampf* (Houghton Mifflin, Boston - 1925)

Keegan, John. *The First World War* (Borzoi Book, New York - 1998)

Longstreet, Stephen. *The Canvas Falcons - The Men and Planes of World War I* (Leo Cooper, London – 1995

Terraine, John. *The Great War, 1914-1918* (Doubleday, New York - 1965)

Lowenherz, H. David, Editor. *The 50 Greatest Letters from America's Wars* (Crown Publishers, New York - 1985)

McConnell, R., James. *Flying for France with the American Escadrille at Verdun* (Doubleday, NewYork - 1916)

Murray, Williamson. *War in the Air, 1914-1945* (Williamson Murray - 1999)

O'Shea, Stephen. *Back to the Front* (Avon Books, New York - 1996)

Paul, Fussell. *The Great War and Modern Memory* (Oxford University Press, London - 1975)

Strachan, Hew. *World War I - A History* (Oxford University Press - 1998)

Weintraub, Stanley. *Silent Night - The Story of the World War I Christmas Truce* (Penguin, New York - 2001)

Wortman, Marc. *The Millionaires' Unit - The Aristocratic Flyboys Who Fought the Great War and Invented American Air Power* (Public Affairs, New York - 2006)

Chapter 2: Tubby

Harcourt, Melville. *The Impudent Dreamer - The Story of Tubby Clayton* (Oxford University Press - 1953)

Clayton, B. P. *Tales of Talbot House – A 'Tubby' Clayton Anthology* (Chatto & Windus - 1919)

Clayton, B. P. 'Tubby' compiled by Durham, John. *Talbot House To Tower Hill* (Toc H, London - 1956)

Chapter 3: Toc H

1919-1929, Ten Years of Toc H, A Picture Book, with a Prologue - The War Years (Toc H - 1929)

Cuttell, Colin. *Ministry Without Portfolio* (Toc H, London - 1962)

Olson, Lynee. *Citizens of London - The Americans Who Stood With Britain In Its Darkest, Finest Hour* (Random House - 2010)

Prideaux-Brune, Kenneth. *Time's Mirror* (Toc H - 1993)

Rice, Judith & Prideaux-Brune, Kenneth. *Out of a Hop Loft - Seventy-Five Years of Toc H* (Darton, Longman & Todd, London –1990)

Toc H, From the First Annual Report. *1919-1929, Ten Years of Toc H - The War Years* (Toc H, London - 1929)

Toc H Journal (Toc H, Volume XV - 1947)

P. B. Clayton. *Plain Tales From Flanders*, (Toc H – 1947)

Chapter 4: Chapter 4: Wayne, C.J. & Toc H
Lynne Olson, *Citizens of London: The Americans Who Stood with Britain in Its Darkest, Finest Hour* (Random House – 2010)

Wayne Kistner Interview, 2/22/2010

Coleman Jennings Interview, 9/4/1976

Correspondence from Coleman Jennings to Wayne Kistner, Dan Irving and John Mitchell, 1976 - 2017

Correspondence and emails from Wayne Kistner, 1976 - 2017

Meetings with Kenneth Prideaux-Brune, London, All Hallows Church, London, England, 2008

Meetings with Hillary Geater, Birmingham, England, 2008

Chapter 5: Amor Ministries – How It All Began
& Chapter 6: The Tijuana Dump
Gayla Cooper Congdon, *Disrupted: Cultivating A Mission – Focused Life* (Standard Publishing 2013)

Scott Congdon Interview: June 12, 2006

Gayla Congdon Interview: June 12, 2006

Scott Horrex Interview, 2007

Correspondence and emails from Scott Congdon, 2006 – 2018

Made in the USA
Las Vegas, NV
15 November 2021